PRELUDE TO THE DIVINE KINGDOM

Divaldo Franco

PRELUDE TO THE DIVINE KINGDOM

By the Spirit
Amélia Rodrigues

ISBN: 978-1-942408-98-7

Original title in Portuguese:
Primícias do Reino
(Brazil, 1967)

Translated by: Ily Reis
Revised by: Andreia M. Netto
Cover design by: Claudio Urpia
Layout: Rones José Silvano de Lima – www.bookebooks.com.br
Edited by: Rones José Silvano de Lima – www.bookebooks.com.br

Edition of
LEAL PUBLISHER
8425 Biscayne Blvd. Ste. 104
Miami, FL 33138, USA
www.lealpublisher.com
(305) 306-6447

Authorized edition by Centro Espírita Caminho da Redenção – Salvador (BA) – Brazil

INTERNATIONAL DATA FOR CATALOGING IN PUBLICATION (ICP)

F895d   Franco, Divaldo (1927)

Prelude to the Divine Kingdom / By Spirit Author Amélia Rodrigues [psychographed by] Divaldo Pereira Franco ; translated by Ily Reis – Miami (FL), USA : Leal Publisher, 2018.

202 p.; 21cm

Original title: *Amanhecer de uma Nova Era*

ISBN: 978-1-942408-98-7

1. Spiritism 2. Psychography 3. Gospel. I Franco, Divaldo Pereira, 1927 – II. Title.

CDD 133.9

CONTENTS

EXPLANATION

At the suggestion of Spirit Benefactors I felt encouraged to provide this preliminary Explanation.

After the sudden disincarnation of one of my brothers on June 24, 1944, in our home town of Feira de Santana (in the state of Bahia, Brazil), and in addition to a series of other painful events, generous hands led me to the acquaintance of a devoted Spiritist[1] medium, Mrs. Ana Ribeiro Borges (Naña). She in turn steered me towards my first mediumistic sessions, during which my psychophonyc[2] aptitude flourished.

A practicing Catholic, for several months I floundered between my old religious convictions and the clear elucidations offered by Spiritism with respect to the mysteries of life, the origins of the being, our trials and destiny through reincarnation.

Sometime later, around 1947, I moved to the capital, Salvador, and under the guidance of supportive Spirit Mentors, started the study of *The Spirits' Book*, by Allan Kardec[3], along

---

[1] Adherents to Spiritism, a Spiritualist Philosophy contained in *The Spirits' Book*, compiled by Allan Kardec, comprised of 1019 questions answered by High Order Spirits. – Tr.

[2] Oral communications of spirits through mediums. – Tr.

[3] Allan Kardec (1804-1869), the Codifier of Spiritism. – Tr.

with the other books of the Spiritist Codification[4]. Not simply reading them, but truly studying them in-depth. From the very start these selfless Instructors from the Spirit World described the Kardecian Codification as most excellent and profound, a depth and excellence I was able to gradually confirm through a systematic and careful assessment that has continued throughout all the years of my life.

In March of 1948, during a vacation at the home of fellow Spiritists in the city of Aracaju, I was invited by the president of the Spiritist Union of Sergipe to speak at their weekly meetings. It was my first public presentation. Stricken by an understandable shyness, I was unable to utter a single word – although the attendees were less than fifteen. During those minutes of torment, which seemed to last forever, I caught a glimpse of a Spirit Friend and heard his blessed voice urging me to "Speak! We will speak for you and with you." My tongue unlocked and movingly and swiftly I "spoke" for almost forty minutes.

That was my initiation to the unpretentious task of evangelical and doctrinal lectures which, by the mercy of God, have continued to this date.

Whenever invited to comment the Gospel I had the impression of seeing the scenes and the personages involved in the narrative, as if they were projected on a cinematic screen. Notwithstanding my limited vocabulary, acting under the control of a strong inspiration I was able – as I still am – to describe these personages and to reproduce their poignant dialogues in emotional and vivid narrations. Other times, to

---

[4] The Spiritist Codification consists of five books compiled by Allan Kardec: *The Spirits' Book, The Mediums' Book, The Gospel according to Spiritism, Heaven and Hell,* and *Genesis.* – Tr.

my utter surprise, I would see myself momentarily outside of my physical body, speaking automatically throughout the whole lecture – a phenomenon that still happens today – without any mental or memory effort, a spectator of my own presentation, amazed at citations and knowledge of facts which, in a normal state, are completely alien to me.

In 1949, while in Muritiba, a town close to Aracaju, at the home of fellow Spiritists, the Rafael Veigas, in a Spiritist session presided by Abel de Mendonça, I felt for the first time a commanding will to write accompanied by a strange sensation on my arm and an anxiety hard to describe. Paper and pencil provided, I wrote swiftly under the same state of mind. That was the starting point, unpretentious and involuntarily, of my psychographic[5] faculty.

Years later, I became more resourceful thanks to the regular practice of my mediumistic abilities at the weekly sessions of the Spiritist Center "Caminho da Redenção" (Pathway to Redemption). At the end of each mediumistic meeting our Spirit Mentors would dictate their comments on the session, invariably encouraging us for the study and practice of Spiritism without superficial embellishment, but according to the substantial teachings of Allan Kardec.

In the same year of 1949, I was regularly delivering small evangelical and doctrinal presentations at this Spiritist Center when these selfless Spirit Mentors – to whom I owe the best teachings of my life, the deepest kindness and constant assistance – suggested an initiative to benefit needy children. That was the start for the plans for the "Mansion of the Way," our blessed workshop of fraternal love. Launched on August

---

[5] Written communications of spirits through mediums (automatic writing). – Tr.

15, 1952, it currently comprises ten "family homes" for 82 parentless children.[6]

Friends and confreres along these many years of evangelical Spiritist presentations have repeatedly asked me to write them down – or at least the topics covered by them. Recognizing my difficulties in the "art of writing" and thus incapable of doing so, I had never harbored such an aspiration. Similar to the lectures, the materials written through me are always dictated by the discarnate Benefactors.

But it just so happened that, less than a year ago, the beloved Spirit Friend Amélia Rodrigues, who on the earth had been a selfless educator, informed me that she had gathered sufficient material for a small book covering several subjects from our past lectures – some of which had been inspired by her in the first place, along with M. Vianna de Carvalho and other workers from the Spirit World. Kindly, and in the presence of participants of the mediumistic sessions of the Spiritist Center "Caminho da Redenção," she conveyed her notes, now gathered in this book, through automatic writing.

Deeply appreciative to Master Jesus for all the blessings that enrich our heart and spirit, we movingly thank the wise and generous Spirit Benefactors for their inspiration and support. At the same time, we ask for the indulgence of the readers that will honor us with their patience and attention, extending our wishes of peace for us all.

DIVALDO PEREIRA FRANCO
Salvador, Bahia, 26 February 1967

---

[6] To this date (2018), the institution has assisted more than 160,000 individuals. – Tr.

PREFACE

"Show me a denarius. Whose image and inscription does it have?"

"In response, they said to him, 'Caesar's'."

"And so, he said to them: "Then repay the things that are Caesar's, to Caesar, and the things that are God's, to God."[7]

Lk. 20:24-25

In this eloquent and expressive dialogue two kingdoms come to a head: the material and the spiritual.

Augustus' effigy and the inscriptions on the coin of purchasing power representing temporal dominance: warrior hosts conquering lands, ephemeral glories of brief duration, bloodied borders stretching everywhere, luxury, debauchery, ambitions, unbridled crime, vanities, and death...

The Emperor, lifted to power through an interminable series of unpredictable events, spread his dominion over all corners of the Empire, his presence felt everywhere, the sound of his coins standing for greatness, affluence, and power.

---

[7] Bible citations taken from the CPDV. – Tr.

The sun never set on the territories of the striking empire.

Jesus, on the other hand, was the Prince of another kingdom, a kingdom of peace and justice where wisdom sublimates aspirations. An immense kingdom beyond-earth, whose pillars nonetheless consubstantiated in the mortar of the earth.

Augustus sowed terror and hatred, ravaging...

Jesus brought the vigorous and straightforward invitation of individual choice, of the highest duty of love.

The former attacked like the eagles: suddenly, with violence, slyness, and impiety.

The latter resembled a gentle dove and was a messenger of peace.

These two kingdoms had and continue to have well-defined purposes and perfectly outlined interests.

Augustus simply reigned. Jesus however, had come to offer the prelude to the Kingdom that would slowly conquer the anguished and disillusioned human spirits, after the failures and frustrations of the fanciful kingdom of ephemeral conquests.

By asking to whom belonged the effigy on the coin, Jesus did not refrain from recognizing the authority of the Emperor, but saw in it an authority granted on the earth and not a legitimate authority that comes from the On High.

* * *

Reflecting on the space programs, the ultra-modern family planning, the daring approaches in youth psychology, the advancements of Sociology with the experimentation of dangerous doctrines, we can no longer ignore the overwhelming surge of lower passions, struggles, and moral wreckage.

At a time when human beings, in spite of all conquests that enrich their experiences, seem to dehumanize themselves, when hurriedness ravages all initiatives, when statistics climb to astonishing heights in all areas of widespread afflictions, when giving hearts and hands are sparse in drying tears, we respectfully wish to convey our appreciation and affection to the Christian-Spiritist groups that fraternally open their doors to the suffering and despair of brothers and sisters, offering shelter and hope under the lofty auspices of the Consoler.[8]

Groups that instruct, enlighten, shelter, console, nourish, illuminate, sustain, and encourage the tormented spirits, victims of their own deeds, their fears, and various neuroses of difficult classification; groups where selfless individuals dedicate their own lives towards the prelude of that kingdom-to-come as "Caesar's" materialism declines, despite the last sparkles of its fading allure; a kingdom whose foundations Jesus came to launch two thousand years ago on the suffering moral grounds of the Planet.

Thinking of these stoic souls, the Christians of the last hour, the sufferers hit and crushed by the tempests of every moment along with those that have not yet struck, we are encouraged to outline some thoughts, studies, and recollections of the "sayings of the Lord" and the personages that took part in His message, presenting it all as an unpretentious invite for the return to the simple, beautiful, and profound topics of the Gospel, nowadays considered polemic, scarcely conveyed, purposely ignored, and violently attacked...

The lack of an evangelical aura in the current so-called Christian endeavors portrays a Christianity that lacks the vigorous and meek, gentle and noble spirit of the Christ.

At a time when Scientism chills the hearts and commands the minds with unusual might, the reminder of Jesus and His life, His words and deeds can be compared to the healing balm gently placed on a mercilessly burning wound.

---

[8]   Spiritism. – Tr.

It is the aim of Spiritism to make individuals strong and pure "like the children" – urging them to be "better today than yesterday and better tomorrow than today."

Our intent is not to present an evangelical exegesis, as we lack the qualifications for such a grand undertaking.

And, on this account, earthly literature is plentiful with the "Lives of Jesus."

Our efforts are focused on lining up a few pages written with care by our immortal spirit after our entrance into the revelatory world beyond the grave. Our objective is to give our contribution to Spiritism's glorious doctrinal works introduced by the eminent master of Lyon[9]. We extend to him our deepest respect and appreciation for his enormous efforts as the restorer of "the living word," through the compilation of the monumental and harmonious Codification in the tumultuous days of the 19th century. Unaltered and ever current, the Codification continues to resist the attacks of frivolity and boastfulness of the reckless in spiritual matters throughout the times.

Some notes that extend beyond the evangelical annotations or impart comments that don't appear in the records of the Good Tidings were extracted by us from research conducted in our sphere of activities in the spirit world, or are the result of clarifications and explanations collected through historical sources on this side of life.

* * *

Similar to the days when Jesus lived amongst us, current times promote the active restoration of the Christian Message. The earth, converted into a laboratory of afflictive experiences, continues to be a field rich with opportunities for evangelical living.

---

[9]   Allan Kardec, born in Lyon, France. – Tr.

There are countless opportunities of service waiting for us.
In these days of culture and abundance, physical and moral
miseries abound waiting for relief.

It is necessary for the seeds of hope to sprout as a spring of
blessings and, as before, that the new "men and women of the
Way" make their presences known everywhere.

Hoping that these humble pages fulfill our call of duty, we
extend our wishes of success to the endeavors of the tireless workers
of the good, recalling in John that Jesus, "the true Light, which
illuminates everyone, was coming into this world" (Jn. 1:9). We
are thus certain that His light illuminates us all, leading us to the
redeeming pathway of His Kingdom of incomparable love.

AMÉLIA RODRIGUES
Salvador, Brazil, 25 February 1967

BITS OF HISTORY

The history of Palestine is more than anything else the tale of a suffering people and their anguished struggle for peace and survival.

Enslaved more than once by the Egyptians, the Babylonians, and other peoples throughout the centuries, after enormous efforts, bloodshed and indescribable suffering, they were finally able to form a communal organization under a theocratic regime – only to unfortunately experience the loss of freedom immediately thereafter.

Instituting the defense of spiritual faith as policy and religion as the foundation of their national identity, they always lived as a closed community under the inspiration of monotheism – an island in a convulsive polytheist sea.

Circa 143 BCE, under the yoke of the Seleucid Empire[10] then at war with Parthians, Romans, Egyptians, and other peoples, Simon Maccabee freed Judea and was subsequently elected general and High Priest by a popular assembly – titles that were retained by heredity in his family, the Hasmoneans.[11]

---

[10] The Seleucid dynasty was founded by Seleucus I, in Persia, in 312 BCE. Around 200 BCE, the Seleucids conquered Syria and the adjacent peoples, at which time Palestine fell under its dominance. – Spirit Auth.

[11] This was called the Second Temple Period, from 142 BCE to 70 CE. – Spirit Auth.

In 78 BCE, Samaria, Galilee, Idumea, Transjordan, and other lands were conquered and added to Judea, allowing Palestine to regain its former borders.

However, while the territorial dimensions grew, the religious fervor diminished. Greek culture had been absorbed by the Hasmonean dynasty, which in turn elicited the harshest disapproval and contempt from the Pharisees.

In 63 BCE, as Pompey and his victorious legions arrived in the East, precisely at the Gates of Damascus, the Israelites invited him to mediate between Hyrcanus II and Aristobulus II[12] in their wrangling for the crown. The mediation favored Hyrcanus. This outcome gave rise to the notorious Pompey campaign against Aristobulus II, who, unhappy with the result, had dared to confront the great Roman general. Losing a battle in the Lower City of Jerusalem, the rebellious prince sought refuge in the Temple in the Upper City, where three months later he was defeated.

Pompey's victory cost the lives of 12,000 Jews and all the lands of the Maccabees, which then fell into the hands of the Roman Empire.

After the death of Crassus, who had plundered the city in 54 BCE, a new insurrection was smothered in blood by Longinus, his successor in the government of Syria. Longinus deported approximately 30,000 Jews, who were reduced to slavery (43 BCE). With the death of Antipater, the triumphant Parthians invaded Jerusalem and turned Antigonus, the last of the Maccabees, into their puppet.

---

[12] Sons of Salome Alexandra, who reestablished the peace with the Pharisees. Before her death, her sons had already started to wage a bitter fight for the throne. – Spirit Auth.

In the meantime, the Second Triumvirate had been established in Rome. Mark Antony and Octavian, in whose hands rested the destinies of the Empire, chose Herod, Antipater's son, to wear the crown of David (40 BCE).

Herod, with an iron grip, expulsed the Parthians, imprisoned Antigonus and delivered him to Antony to be put to death; furthermore, to make himself feared and obeyed unquestionably, he ordered the killing of all the Jews who had supported the invaders.

With Herod, the Greek splendor reached its golden age in Israel.

Dazzling cities emerged, sculptures sprouted all over, monuments and grand buildings enriched Jerusalem's landscape, theaters and circuses were erected and athletic competitions, musical contests, gladiators' fights introduced.

In Caesarea a sea port was built; Byblos, Rhodes, Sparta, and Athens were greatly enhanced...

Deeming the Temple of Jerusalem built by Zerubbabel as devoid of the splendor worthy of Israel, Herod had it knocked down, erecting in its place a grander and more imposing building.

As dissolute and ambitious as he was unmerciful, Herod killed anyone who disputed his authority, sparing neither Aristobulus, legitimate heir to the throne (causing him to be drowned while bathing in a pool) nor Marianme, his second wife, granddaughter of Hyrcanus II and sister to Aristobulus. Some of his own sons, Alexander for instance, died in the hands of his henchmen, whereas Antipater, considered a suspect in a conspiracy, was imprisoned indefinitely.

Any hint of sedition was drowned in blood. The circle of spies was so widespread that one day, while roaming in disguise among the people, Herod asked a man his opinion about the king and got this reply: "In Jerusalem even the ravens are spies."

* * *

In 4 CE, stricken with edema, fevers, and ulcers Herod finally died, bequeathing the House of Israel to his three sons: Herod Philip II, Herod Antipas, and Herod Archelaus.

The funeral rites at the Herodium were scarcely over when the very ambitious 18 year-old Archelaus, after suppressing an uprising, traveled to Rome to seek Augustus' support to reign absolute.

Herod Antipas, after implementing some measures, also traveled to Italy.

Herod Philip II fled to the north and settled there safely.

Rome, by order of the Emperor, applied its customary policy toward the conquered people, that is, to further weaken them through their own internal fights and disputes. Thus, Archelaus became the ethnarch of Judea; Herod Philip and Herod Antipas were made tetrarchs – the former for the cities of Gaulanitis, Trachonitis, Batanea, and Paneas, and the latter for Galilee and Perea, including the cities of Nazareth and Esdrelon...

Herod Philip I, the firstborn, grandson of the High Priest on his maternal side, had been radically and definitely disinherited. He tried to wear the "White Mitre" and the "breastplate of faith," but remained instead a simple priest while the highest function was retained by brothers of his grandfather.

* * *

The Lake of Gennesaret, due to the beauty of its shores and fresh breezes, had been designated by the Rabbis as the place "Elohim had reserved for his own pleasure." It was quite natural, therefore, that the two tetrarchs would choose it to build the capital-city of their domains. More powerful in weapons and money than his brother, Antipas erected the famed Tiberias – so named in honor of the Roman Emperor – partly on the site of an old cemetery, to the dismay of the orthodox Jews who considered it "impure."

Herod Philip, on the other hand, took hold of the old city of Paneas, located on the mouth of the Jordan River and the lake, almost leaning over the water. He beautified and greatly improved it, changing its name to "Caesarea Philippi."

In Rome, after meeting with the Emperor, Archelaus had been bestowed the best chunk, comprised of Samaria, Idumea, and Judea, with Jerusalem as the capital of his domains. Equal to his father in cruelty and shrewdness, he increased the taxes and reconstructed cities with the sweat and tears of his subjects. Deaf to the reiterated pleas of the people to reduce their oppression, a subsequent insurgency was crushed in blood. The internal dissatisfaction continued, however, now redirected towards the Roman domination. After the Emperor was notified of the calamitous situation by a committee of prestigious Jews, Archelaus fell into disgrace. Augustus deposed him, forcing Archelaus to settle in Gaul (in the city of Vienne) with an order to not move from there (6 CE).

At around this time, a Roman procurator was designated for Jerusalem.

The rebellion, however, did not abate, prompting the Romans to act with force, crucifying 2,000 Jews to consolidate their victory.

* * *

Jesus lived his infancy as a subject of Herod Antipas.

At the start of His public ministry, Palestine was under the supervision of Syria, whose legate was Pomponius Flaccus, while the Roman procurator of Judea was Pontius Pilate, the fifth in the succession.

From his palace in Caesarea Maritima, Pilate controlled everything.[13]

Under the Roman oppression, Israel was comprised of three distinct social classes, divided in varying social, religious, and political segments, as well as numerous other sects – among them the Essenes, who abided by the tenet that "what is mine is yours," and known for their austerity, gentleness, and fraternity.

The Council of Elders, consisting of 72 members, among them the High Priest, legislated over the life and death of its subjects.

The Sadducees (*Zadokim* – so named after Zadok, their leader and founder), comprised of the feudal aristocracy in charge of the religious ministries, were zealous followers of the rigorous applications of the Law or Torah. Invariably wealthy, they enjoyed consideration and deference.

The Pharisees (*Perushim* – separatists), considered economically independent, constituted the middle class; they believed themselves to be "more Jewish than the Jews," keeping the strict orthodox requirements in their religious practices as initially introduced by the Maccabees.

---

[13] To govern these 2 million people at the time (it was assumed that there were approximately 100,000 Jews in Jerusalem) Rome kept 3,000 men divided in three infantry cohorts and one cavalry contingent in addition to various aids recruited among the Syrians, Samarians, Greeks, and Arabs. – Spirit Auth.

The common folk (*Am Ha-aretz* – people of the land), a blend of beggars, weavers, workhands, artisans of all kinds, small farmers, all reduced to extreme poverty by the harrying taxes, comprised the "proletariat" (as Rome designated them). These common folk were hated, persecuted, and despised by all the other classes.

Without any rights, stigmatized by general hatred, the *Am Ha-aretz* filled the countryside and the cities. Jerusalem and Rome alike had their fill of the "jobless," but in Rome the Emperor at least gave them "bread and circus," keeping them fed and entertained. The *Am Ha-aretz* united under a faction, the *fanatics*, later divided into Zealots and Sicarii. Rioters, they persecuted the Jews who sympathized with the Romans, sometimes stabbing them in public squares. Spreading terror, they incited an uprising, destroying hamlets and villages that refused to follow them.

The Pharisees, out of convenience, appeared to accept Roman rule, although detesting the Romans who in turn despised them as well.

Rome, through its procurators, insisted in placing the symbols of its power in the Temple of Jerusalem: the dominating eagle or the statue of the Emperor, any of which provoked bloody reactions.

The scuffles, however, changed from a political motivation into a religious character when Theudas, a mix of messiah and liberator, in trying to repeat Moses' achievement at the Red Sea, led some followers to the Jordan River, only to be massacred by the Romans who also killed the pseudo messiah…

In 66 CE, a new wave of insurgencies erupted with little success for the Jews. Once more beaten and defeated, peace was bought by the Pharisee Rabbi Johanan ben Sakkai, thereby saving the wealth of the wealthy. However, small merchants, artisans, and "people of the land," unhappy with this outcome, invaded and looted the royal palace, a fight that continued until the complete destruction of the Temple in 70 CE by the order of Titus, killing more than 600,000 insurgents all over Palestine.

Around 132 CE, under the command of Simon bar Kokhba, who called himself the *Redeemer*, the Jews attempted a new revolt, which brought them final defeat with Simon's death in Bethar.

The Romans killed more than 500,000 Jews, destroying more than 900 villages. The price for an Israelite slave was reduced to less than what was paid for a horse.

Subsequently, Emperor Hadrian prohibited any and all Jewish religious or civil acts throughout the entire Roman Empire. As a result, after the disastrous Kokhba revolt, the "elected people" were made to endure a dolorous diaspora throughout the centuries.

Meanwhile, a new pagan city, Aelia Capitolina, with its Roman customs and lifestyles, was built on top of the ashes of Jerusalem…

Never before had a people suffered such a long and cruel exile!

* * *

Amid this climate of hatred of all kinds, amid the most pungent sufferings, Jesus spread love, liberty, and peace, announcing the Kingdom of God and preaching non-violence up to His ultimate sacrifice on the cross. Setting the purposes of life on "the love for God above all things and the love for our neighbors as we love ourselves," He left this luminous and supreme legacy of love to all humankind.

CHAPTER 1

THE GOOD TIDINGS

The coming of Jesus into the coarse fluids of the terrestrial orb reflects the story of redemption of humanity itself, departing from the dark labyrinths of the individual "me" towards the higher pinnacles of liberty.

Living during the reigns of Augustus and Tiberius, whose lives left strong marks in History, His cradle and His tomb forever marked the times, becoming civilization's dividing feature – the predominating event in the annals of human life.

Accepting as His cradle a humble barn during the significant time of a census, from the very start He epitomized a profound lesson of humility, presenting a *different kingdom* to humankind at a time when the supremacy of might enthroned the sword, and the imperial mantle covered the lands over which the victors marched.

He never wavered from His initial objective: to be a servant to all.

Charting the maddening march of the human spirit, bound to successive cycles of rebirths amid enslaving passions, He had pioneers and emissaries from His celestial dwelling precede Him, singing the lofty glories of life and beauty, conveying dreams of ascension and sublime expectations...

* * *

Before His coming:

Hammurabi expands the limits of his land by cruel wars and writes a code in stone tablets, the first humanity had ever heard of...

Krishna renews the doctrine of the Vedas, whose origins are lost in the folds of the centuries, and preaches the immortality of the spirits and their successive lives...

Akhenaton introduces significant reforms in Egyptian worship, inspired by lofty thoughts...

Abraham, psychically connected to the spirit world, leaves the city of Ur and becomes a father again...

Moses, in communion with High Order Spirits, frees the Jews from slavery, *receives* the Decalogue, and brings to the world the idea of One God only...

Siddhartha Gautama endeavors to reach Paradise and enlightens himself, illuminating the earth with incomparable lessons of self-denial, peace, and harmony...

K'ung Fu-tzu (Confucius) emphasizes morality, fidelity and family, and renews concepts of life...

Lao Tzu writes the *Book of the Way and Its Virtue* (Tao Te Ching) based on his experience, self-denials, and deep meditations...

Pythagoras, at his admirable school in Croton, after complex initiation advocates high morals, austerity, and preaches the doctrine of rebirths...

Socrates synthesizes the ideas of the East and initiates the period of a noble Philosophy, rooted in the highest morality and the immortality of the soul...

... And so many others tread the earth, some triumphant, many defeated, expanding the horizons of the earth for His arrival...

... Alcibiades sings the Muses, while fomenting war.

Periander rises as one of the seven sages of Greece, but commits ignoble uxoricide...

Julius Caesar harnesses the chariots of destruction to his wrists, and elevates himself to the heights of divinity...

Alexander the Great conquers the world, but is unable to intimidate the Gymnosophists[14] who inhabited the banks of the Indus River. Fond of Homer, he states that in the *Iliad* he found the inspiration for love and war, bringing him so many glories... But he too passes quickly, at 33, after having lived what could amount to many lives...

Rights always pertain to the conquerors, the common folk nothing more than beasts of burden in the claws of the mighty.

After His passage, Marcus Aurelius records the thoughts that flow from his privileged mind under the lofty inspiration of Wise Emissaries while battling in fields covered with corpses; wild hosts, under the guise of political hegemony of vandals risen to power, sweep through like scorching and blazing human fires, their legions leaving only destruction, ashes, and the devastation of destroyed and bereaved cities ...

The ephemeral victors erect monuments to their folly, with arrogance qualifying as victory – tributes that will tumble down once the triumphant are gone...

... Everything comes and goes! The Great Sphinx consumes everything...

Refulgent thrones, impressive official titles, resplendent cohorts under the sun, grand conquests, golden and ruthless civilizations, everything disappears over time...

---

[14] Gymnosophists – Indian philosophers who refrained from eating meat, dedicating themselves to mystical contemplation. "Naked philosophers." – Spirit Auth.

He on the other hand arrives silently, pure, and stays.

He gathers the masses of the afflicted and shelters them close to His heart.

He asks for nothing, He demands nothing.

A liberator par excellence, He sings the hymn of true liberty, preaching the breaking of the inferior links that fasten humankind to the cruelest chains...

He immerses Himself in flesh, but is a Sun of incomparable light, illuminating the fulcrum of millennia.

To the gentle sound of His voice hope awakens and forgotten ideals resume.

To His compelling words the day rises and the future pulsates, sending into the core of the world the foundations of the Blissful Humanity to come.

He admonishes and He helps.

He reproaches vehemently and He succors.

He accepts the offering of love but does not imprison the truth in the walls of subornment.

A Celestial King, He partakes in the necessities of wrongdoers and lives among them.

He exchanges the contact with the angels for the communion with the populace of the green and calm Capernaum, trading the splendors of the Milky Way for the crimson dawns of the fish-abundant lake.

He prefers the sweltering evenings of Jericho to the celestial spectacle of the stars in infinite sunlit splendor.

He takes in the dust of the parched and solitary roads of Canaan, Magdala, Dalmanutha. He narrows His cosmic frontiers, concealed in the depth of the solar system, to the confines between the Sea and Hebron, Syria and the Land of Moab...

He leaves the paradisiacal dwelling to pick a seed of mustard and with it create a cantata under the stifling heat;

hungry, He asks a fig tree for fruits which, out of season, it cannot provide...

Lord of the World – He who already was before the world's creation – He mingles with the multitudes, the ragged crowd, that feverishly search for love unable to identify it; indeed He lives in the midst of the masses, where in suffering He finds the reason for His glorious martyrdom.

Among the afflicted He expresses the most eloquent words humankind has ever heard.

His Good Tidings are woven with the spontaneous musicality of Nature, in the scenery of spring times and summer times, around villages and the lake, in the exuberant heart of the burgeoning Earth...

Betrayed, wounded, crucified, He selects a serene and luminous morning to reappear, seeking out a formerly possessed woman to tell her that life does not cease, that the Kingdom of God is inside the heart, reaffirming indisputably that He will stay "with us every day until the end of times." He then returns to the Father, where He awaits for us after we succeed in our fervent liberating struggles for ascension.

CHAPTER 2

THE PRECURSOR

Screeching on its worn-out hinges, the door opened and a grotesque figure appeared in the doorsill, raising a shining curved sword towards the swath of moonlight creeping into the narrow prison cell.[15]

The quiet night is bathed in silvery light, and the muffled sounds of the bacchanal taking place beyond its walls can be heard every so often.

Machaerus or the Macheronte of Roman times, the gloomy fortress erected on the top of the plateau of Moab, in Perea, bared unlimited vistas. On one side the Dead Sea, approximately 1,200 meters[16] below, and farther away, beyond the vast plains, Mount Nebus, from where Moses glimpsed the Promised Land.

In that tower of the sinister citadel he had already endured ten months of dolorous captivity.

He had not been tortured, that was true; but isolated from his beloved disciples – to whom he preached the need

---

[15] Mt. 3:1-12 and 14:1-2; Mk. 1:1-8 and 6:14-29; Lk. 3:1-20 and 9:7-9; Jn. 1:19-37. – Spirit Auth.
[16] App. 4,000 feet. – Tr.

for repentance and penitence at the ford of Bethabara or the "springs of peace" of Sythopolis – he suffered the anguish of undue imprisonment. Silently, he recalled his words to his supporters when they, somewhat jealous, spoke to him about Jesus:

"A man is not able to receive anything, unless it has been given to him from heaven. You yourselves offer testimony for me that I said, 'I am not the Christ,' but that I have been sent before him. He who holds the bride is the groom. But the friend of the groom, who stands and listens to Him, rejoices joyfully at the voice of the groom. And so, this, my joy, has been fulfilled. He must increase, while I must decrease…"

* * *

It was March 29 CE.

Herod Antipas was returning from a journey to Babylon as a member of the Tiberius entourage headed by the legate Vitellius. The trip had been undertaken to seek the support of Artabanus, king of the Medes, who had defeated the Parthians in a cruel and bloody war.

Unusually held back in Machaerus during that winter time – a period he invariably spent enjoying the lovely climate of Tiberias – Herod decided to offer a sumptuous feast for the princely and idle retinue in celebration of his birthday.

* * *

The prisoner knew that moment would come and thus had sought strength in long and serene meditations.

In these months of bitter captivity, he maintained a strong spirit and unbroken courage. He never wavered, he never doubted. If he had many lives, he would give them all at once for the right to announce the days of justice to come and to decry the dissipation of customs that had pervaded the royal court, where rampant incest and adultery were accepted under a mundane condescending indulgence.

In his past pilgrimages through the desert, eating frugally while immersed in deep thought, he had felt the strong and intangible hands of the Father giving him strength. He also had *heard* in his heart the wordless voices of angelic beings urging him to preach redemption, so as to open the pathways through which the Awaited One would tread...

That was the hour of his testimony, he could feel it.

Clammy and cold, he knew what was to come as he recalled all the moments of his life.

Mentally he returned to the happy days of his childhood, clouded only by his growing inner concerns regarding God and humankind, worries that greatly intensified in his youth.

How many times – he could not tell – after listening to the narratives of the Law in the synagogue or commenting the Sacred Texts he would feel the need to meditate on his own, lost in the arid and parched roads in the harsh regions of the mountainous and scorching desert! And in doing so, how many inextricable visions he had! ... In all the worries that beleaguered him and in all the necessities he sought to elude, he felt that the Heavens steered him toward one destiny only: to prepare the pathways for someone else to walk on... the Liberating Messiah!

Everything in his life had been unusual starting with his transcendental birth at a time his parents no longer expected a child.

He knew well of his origin as told by his father Zechariah himself.

Anxious for a child, his father had gone to the Temple to pray and was surprised by the presence of a spiritual being who told him: "Do not be afraid, Zechariah, for your prayer has been heard, and your wife Elizabeth shall bear a son to you. And you shall call his name John."

A great fear engulfed his father and a strange muteness struck him, but at last the birth of his son came to be.

The hands of God undoubtedly were laid upon his home.

Time went by...

Grown up, on his way to the desert, like the ancient prophet Elijah, he wore clothing of camel's hair and a leathern girdle round his loins...

He had started his ministry around the year 15 of the empire of Tiberius Caesar, while Pontius Pilate was the governor of Judea and Herod Antipas the tetrarch of Galilee...

He had come all the way down from the harsh and rocky plateaus of Perea to Bethabara, close to the mouth of the Dead Sea, where the Jordan River creates a ford that facilitates the crossing of the caravans. He had started there, preaching and cleansing the spirit's *impurities* with the water of the river, while expecting the One who would ultimately lead humankind, anointing it with the fire of truth, the sign of eternal life.

Winter time there is delightful with river waters rushing by, singing among garlands of tall reed and large ferns, under the shade of the tamarinds whose greenness contrasts with the scorching bare desert farther out...

At 30 years of age, he was at the peak of strength and vigor.

His thunderous voice could be heard without ceasing: "For even now the axe has been placed at the root of the trees. Therefore, every tree that does not produce good fruit shall be cut down and cast into the fire."

The recollection brings tears to his eyes: a deep longing for the days spent in preparation of His coming...

* * *

Almost five centuries had gone by without any prophetic voices, and an overall apprehension had set into people's hearts.

The blood of the victims of the unending wars and scuffles smothered by fire and sword flowed abundantly, and the clamor of the voices towards the Lord were deafening. The Heavens, however, remained silent...

Undoubtedly, he felt he was the "lone voice in the wilderness" preparing "the way for the Lord." That had been his response to the Jews sent by the priests and Levites of Jerusalem when he was asked if he was the Christ or Elijah who was to come. At that moment an unusual force had come over him and in a righteous tone of voice he proclaimed: "Indeed, I baptize you with water for repentance, but He who will come after me is more powerful than me. I am not worthy to carry His sandals." It had taken place in Bethany, somewhat away from the river, and he had felt powerful in his smallness.

The next day – he recalled with eyes clouded with tears and an indescribable inner elation – dawn had spread slowly over the land and the "House of the Way" had been swarming with visitors. Under the blossoming tamarinds and oleanders a myriad of insects buzzed about while sweet fragrances scented the air.

He had been preaching the coming of the Kingdom of God with unusual emotion.

His forceful delivery – words flowing in cascades of consoling hope – moistened his eyes burning from the scorching sun. As he moved about in his eagerness to enlist souls for his cause, he caught sight of Him descending the green slope of the river, His garments uncommonly bright, His head covered in the traditional keffiyeh.[17] The makeshift vessel used for the pouring of water slid from his hand and he cried out, unable to contain himself: "Behold, this is the One about whom I said, 'After me arrives a man, who has been placed ahead of me, because He existed before me. And I did not know Him. Yet it is for this reason that I come baptizing with water: so that He may be made manifest in Israel."

And approaching the newcomer, he said:

"I ought to be baptized by You, and yet You come to me?"

"Permit this for now. For in this way it is fitting for us to fulfill all justice."

He spoke with eloquent spiritual greatness.

After the simple act a voice was heard, if from inside or outside the spirit he could not say in his recollection: "This is my beloved son in whom I am well pleased."

Everything had happened in January the previous year, and yet it still seemed so near!...

... And then He left through the same trail used by the sheep, disappearing amid the rows of tamarinds. He never saw Him again, he never had the bliss of talking to Him again.

A serene trust had taken over his spirit since that day.

He started to more fervently proclaim the moral dissipation wherever he would find it.

He went to see the Tetrarch and reproached his conduct.

How could that coward and ignoble contemptible king betray the daughter of Aretas, king of the Nabateans, forcing her to seek asylum with her father in Petra, beyond Perea,

---

[17]   A type of turban. – Spirit Auth.

while he took the wife of his half-brother, Herod Phillip I – who lived in Rome as a citizen without any titles – a woman who was also the daughter of another half-brother, Aristobulus, passionate like his grandmother, Marianme the Hasmonean, murdered by Herod the Great!...

The words stung, deeply impressing Antipas.

But, weak or indifferent, not reacting at all, the king did not have the nobility to free himself from this strange passion.

He, on the other hand, was well aware of the wrath that consumed the soul of the woman he reproved, wounded in her pride and arrogance...

Night time had fallen, the cold winds blowing over the hills of Gilead.

* * *

The high-pitched fifes pierce the starry night while the shadows in the fortress great hall dance under the red flames of the hanging copper and crystal lamps...

Memories continue to flood his mind in the cold and pestilent dungeon.

So many humiliations, which in reality did not hurt him!

Inwardly he remembered: "He must increase, while I must decrease..." He so much would have loved to have heard and to have talked to the Anointed One! He remembered the anguish of Moses, who saw the "promised land" from the heights of Mt. Nebus but was unable to reach it...

With this fear in his heart, perhaps born in the days of solitary and gloomy captivity, he had sent two of his disciples in search of Jesus, of Whom he had heard so many things, to make inquiries...

Yet he had received no response and his time had come. Profuse sweat covered his body.

But he was at peace.

His spirit, prepared for the testimony, had no illusions. He had forged his hope in the bellows, furnaces and anvils of asceticism, total dedication, and trust.

He stood up, breathed in the quiet night air, gazed at the swath of embroidered sky bathed in moonlight, and turned to the executioner who sternly observed him through the open door. His voice sounded as firm as in the past despite his physical exhaustion.

"I'm ready!" He said.

He kneeled on the filthy straw of his cell, and bowed his head toward the floor.

* * *

Some months before, on a clear morning in lovely Galilee, the disciples of John the Baptist anxiously asked the strange and noble Rabbi:

"Are you He who is to come, or should we expect another?"

"Go and report to John what you have heard and seen: that the blind see, the lame walk, the lepers are cleansed, the deaf hear, the dead rise again, the poor are evangelized. And blessed is anyone who has not taken offense at me."

The disciples left soon thereafter, moved and enraptured. The Master, filled with tenderness for the prisoner who had sent them to speak to Him, said:

"What did you go out to the desert to see? A reed shaken by the wind? So what did you go out to see? A man in soft garments? Behold, those who are clothed in soft garments are in the houses of kings. Then what did you go out to see? A prophet? Yes, I tell you, and more than a prophet. For this is he, of whom it is written: 'Behold, I send my Angel before your face, who shall prepare your way before you'."

The revelation coming from the lips of the Rabbi is framed in pristine beauty as He continues:

"Truly I say to you, among those born of women, there has arisen no one greater than John the Baptist. Yet the least in the kingdom of heaven is greater than he. But from the days of John the Baptist, even until now, the kingdom of heaven has endured violence, and the violent carry it away. For all the prophets and the law prophesied, even until John. And if you are willing to accept it, he is the Elijah, who is to come. Whoever has ears to hear, let him hear."

Indeed, John is Elijah reincarnated, opening the routes and preparing the pathways!

The truth is stated. A new Light is cast over the labyrinths of multimillenary ignorance.

* * *

At the Machaerus celebration, mingling with guests from everywhere, were Herodias and Salome, Herodia's daughter from her marriage to Herod Philip I[18]; Agrippa, Herodia's brother – who under Emperor Caligula would be designated the successor to Phillip and, after Antipas' exile to Lugdunum in Gaul, would succeed him as Tetrarch; and Herod Philip II, the peaceful Tetrarch of Gaulanitis and Trachonitis, soon to be married to Salome.

---

[18] Also called Herod II. – Tr.

The feast, worthy of the courts of the East, exceeded in opulence and excitement.

Arriving in his luxurious litter, surrounded by an entourage of his minions and servants, Vitellius was triumphantly received by the birthday bash host.

Crotales reverberated; zithers and kinnors filled the air with languid and exotic melodies while cymbals set the feverish beat.

Lamps in all their splendor, candleholders in silver and gold, poured their light over rugs from Babylon, Tyre, and Sidon, while colorful fabrics from Damascus hung over the walls of carved stone.

Hyacinths, dahlias, roses and jasmine intertwined in colorful fragrant garlands were hung all around the richly carved ebony and mahogany tables.

Sadducees and Pharisees talked animatedly while succulent delicacies are paraded around and offered to the guests.

A slave sings a mysterious, foreign melody.

During an interval, the hangings are flung open.

Suddenly, to everyone's astonishment, teenage girl Salome starts to dance...

The wine flows freely and the impassioned dancing inebriates the princes, the Pharisees, and all other guests.

The dance, a mixture of religious and pagan rhythms, is lascivious.

As the music stops and a triumphant silence follows, the dancer drops to the floor in an unusual and lustful motion.

Antipas, intoxicated by wine and sensuality, exclaims feverishly, wrapping his arms around the young girl:

"Ask! Ask for half of my kingdom and I shall give it you!"

The ambitious mind of the excited teenager is filled with the passions and expectations of her time.

Surprised, she seeks out her mother for advice and Herodias, taking advantage of the occasion, whispers to her: ask him for John's head.

The girl turns pale.

Her mother insists tyrannically: "Ask! Ask and I will give you anything you want. This man John dared disrespect me in front of the rabble and the king himself, who like a coward superstitious Edomite did not have the guts to punish him, to behead him to serve as an example. Clean my name, my child! I'm not only asking you, I'm demanding it!"

The air was thick, the expectations heavy.

Someone shouted: "Ask him! He is the king, and once he promises he won't be able to retract. We are the witnesses. Ask him!"

With a throaty voice, the young girl asks:

"Give me the head of John so that I can dance!"

Antipas, however, respected and feared the Baptist.

Hearing the peculiar request he trembled, his face ashen.

Loud laughter exploded in the air, all voices in one prodding him:

"Give her the head of the Baptist – or are you afraid of it?!"

Dazed, the king calls one of his henchmen, ordering him to cut off John's head in his cell.

High above in the sky the half-moon hid behind dark clouds while an anxious gloomy silence sets in…

* * *

… The silver blade cuts through the air, and with a thump the head of the Precursor rolls on the stone floor…

The music starts again and twirling, holding a silver tray, Salome hands Herodias the trophy: the head of the

Baptist, whose lightless eyes gaze at the cruel conscience of his executioners.

Deranged, the wretched woman starts to laugh…

Elijah, reincarnated as John the Baptist, had paid for his crime on the banks of the Kishon River, where he, Elijah, had ordered the beheading of the worshipers of Baal. His spirit, free after fulfilling his mission, ascended towards the Heavens.

John's disciples pleaded Antipas for his body and buried it with care.

On a distant hill, listening to the silent night, Jesus prayed.

A few days later, He left the domains of Herod Antipas to sow the good tidings in other lands…

The Scriptures had been fulfilled.

The Precursor had become silent so that the Messiah's voice would be heard all over the earth, signaling a new Era.

CHAPTER 3

SUBLIME HYMN

That month of June had been hotter than in previous years.[19]

The long airless day withered away while the sun, half hidden behind the towering peaks, seared the vaporous passing clouds from its carriage sprinkled with purple and gold.

The gently sloped mountain ended in a large plateau dotted with trees that, no matter how small, offered shelter and protection.

Since earlier in the day anxious multitudes had flocked there, drawn by high expectations. They were Galileans from the region nearby: fishermen, farmers, humble and suffering folk, burdened and afflicted. They were Jews from Jordan, from Jerusalem, and foreigners from the Decapolis. Regional dialects blended in the air, all united in an immense curiosity rising from anticipation and hope.

Oppressed by the mighty, they invariably suffered their arrogance and conceited disdain.

Mutually dependent, they loved each other in their suffering and need.

---

[19] Mt. 5:1-48; Mt. 6:1-34; Mt. 7:1-29; Mt. 6:17-49. – Spirit Auth.

That Rabbi who consoled them was the King tenderly awaited for many centuries who would free them from shame and servitude...

They had seen and heard Him more than once. No one before had ever done what He did, or had spoken as He spoke.

They came from everywhere: from the lake area and the fields, from distant cities and villages just to hear Him.

There was something special in the air.

The golden blue skies floated over the burned green color of the earth, a caressing breeze alternatively blowing from the sea or the slopes and buttresses of Mt. Hermon, spreading the bittersweet scent of the parched soil over the vast plain of Esdrelon.

* * *

The mountain, with its distinctive grandeur, is also a symbol: the *Son of Man* who comes down to humankind, overcoming the difficulties of the immersion into the abyss, and the *Man* who rises, guiding humankind from the lacerating steep cliff up, towards the bosom of God.

A mountain is also a majestic landmark on the landscape.

To climb, to go up a mountain, suggests the overcoming of obstacles that hinder advance on the evolutionary journey. To come down, to leave the mountain, means not to be deterred by difficulties and to retrace your path, stretching out hands towards those who remained behind...

The descent towards humankind to lift it to God is very arduous.

To mingle with human conflicts to find the spirits lost in the darkness of their apparent necessities; to glow afterwards in a sublime dawn, guiding them over the ashes of yesterday so that they can reach the plateau where the sun of the clear and awaited Day shines everlastingly...

To descend without falling.

Human beings raise obstacles where opinions abound, and erect mountains where conventions exist.

To forget about oneself and come down towards those wallowing in petty concerns vitalized by greed and emotional unbalance.

To give oneself, to integrate in a way that is common to all but not equal to any.

There's the diptych: to ascend; to descend.

To ascend without forsaking the valleys and to descend without forgetting the Summits.

The mountain was just any mountain.

The poem that would be sung there had never been heard before, and shall never be heard again in any time alike...

* * *

Matthew the Evangelist asserts that "Then, seeing the crowds, He ascended the mountain" while Luke states that "And descending with them, He stood in a level place..."

Ascending or descending! It is of no matter.

The truth is that He stopped on the plain of the mount and as He stood there ...

... He became resplendent.

A radiant halo lit up his hair, stirred by the light breeze, luminescent.

The sweltering garments and the anxiety of the world all around. In the multitudes men, women, and children that would keep in their minds and their hearts the Message, the Poem dividing different realities.

The multitudes were His passion, His life. To love them and to tend to them, that was His reason.

Seeing the multitudes docile and drawn to Him, forgetting about themselves in a sublime communion extending beyond this life, He opened his mouth, and taught them by saying:

"Blessed are the poor in spirit, for theirs is the kingdom of heaven!"

They poor, they knew Him well: the raggedy, the foul-smelling, the sick, all stretching out hands that misery shrivels.

They were poor indeed – but how many of them still carried the embodiments of *richness* in their spirit! A spirit *rich* in rebelliousness, lower passions, a large reservoir of anguish and bitterness…

Thus, who would be the "poor in spirit"?

The wind blows a gentle singsong around the meditative multitude, left pondering in the spontaneous silence and long pause that follow…

The rich possess coins and titles, properties and spirits rich with ambition, pride, and misoneism.

The "poor in spirit" are free from possessions and ambitions, they love freedom, they fight for human rights, they are idealists, lovers of the truth, and they are prepared for the truth.

No shackles tied to the past, no tantalizing enticements lurking ahead.

Reminiscent to the simple, the unadorned, the children.

Totally free.

Aspirants to the Kingdom of God and its subjects already.

Innocent because they triumphed at the cost of tears and sweat. Their debts paid, their wounds washed and therefore now pure, without the emptiness of the "I," predisposed to self-liberation, to self-sublimation.

Freed from the residues of the world, not absorbed, not afflicted. With everyone, next to everyone, without anyone, not tied to others, to the conventions of others.

"Poor in spirit!"

* * *

The multitude awaits; hearts beat with anticipation; eyes sparkle with a different glow.

The voice of the Rabbi continues the poem:

"Blessed are those who mourn, for they shall be consoled!"

"The lamp of your body is your eye." All eyes glisten, filled with tears.

The figure of the Rabbi is golden, reflected against the clear distant sky.

Everybody there had shed tears, some unceasingly, hidden or openly, in their harsh trials.

Long is the road of suffering, harsh and cruel the days of their lives.

Spirits marked by apprehension and worries, hearts broken, sickness and expiations...

They all weep and experience the renewing peace that comes from tears.

Many believe that weeping is shameful, forgetting that there are tears of shame.

Others say that tears are a flaw that reveals weakness and indignity.

Rain unburdens the clouds and enriches the soil; it washes away the mud and vitalizes the orchard.

Tears convey the divine presence.

When someone weeps, the divine Law is at work, opening pathways of future peace in the provinces of the spirit.

Tears, however, should not unleash rebelliousness for outbursts of folly, nor flow in torrents that break down the barriers of equilibrium like a tumultuous stream that sows destruction and devastates the fields.

To weep is to seek God in the bleak regions of solitude.

Alone and next to Him.

Forgotten by all, remembered by Him.

Shed everywhere, heard by His ears.

Weeping says what the mouth does not dare to whisper.

Someone weeping is imploring, is waiting.

Unable to express themselves in words, to bare their souls, to rid themselves of all disquiet.

… "They shall be consoled!"

* * *

West winds spread the pollen of small flowers in the valley below, while the flanks of the rocks channel the singing air.

The multitude is filled with hope.

The Master, speaking slowly to penetrate all minds, affirms vigorously:

"Blessed are the meek for they shall inherit the earth!"

* * *

The earth has always belonged to the mighty who couple impiety with astuteness, ready to crush, trouncing the timid and meek.

The disciples look at each other…

But meekness is the halo of peace, the sibling of equilibrium.

The heirs to the earth receive it covered in blood, a sea strewn with carcasses; they are also heirs, all of them, of the hatred and repulse of the conquered.

The meek are the owners of the earth that no one can seize, the home that no one can defile, the land where goods abound and the blessings are bountiful.

"They shall inherit the earth!"

* * *

The serene and tranquil afternoon is crystal-clear.

Unknown vibrations bring music to the vast wavy and colorful landscape.

The expressive words of the Master sing yet another theme of the Incomparable Symphony:

"Blessed are those who hunger and thirst for justice, for they shall be satisfied!" Hunger and thirst for justice!

The procession of uncaught criminals is infinite and unending.

The chariots of warriors and vandals speed over defeated cities, orphans, and forsaken widows.

Injustice dwells in the hearts, and the indifference of lawmakers and rulers is almost complicity.

The world is burning with thirst for justice.

Men and women collapse, hungry, at the doors of Justice.

The foolhardy, however, resume their former way, reincarnating in the grips of madness and marked by cruelty.

Blessed are those who suffer their atrocities.

There is a hope that is life for the thirsty and hungry.

Open sores, wounds to the heart, overlooked injuries claiming relief from the justice of love.

The anguished man and woman at the doors of the Truth.

Truth descending towards them, enlightening and pacifying.

Reborn to redeem, recommencing to rectify, repeating experiences to learn.

Judged by conscience, corrected by love, set for liberation.

"They shall be satisfied!"

* * *

A steadfast equilibrium brings serenity to the multitude.

Jesus is the hyphen of light – the convergence point – between two worlds in conflict: the spiritual and the material.

Men and women on the mount get closer to each other, look at each other, identify with each other.

Involving them all with an expressive gaze of compassion and understanding, Jesus enlightens:

"Blessed are the merciful, for they shall obtain mercy!"

Mercy towards others is a light that one casts on one's own path, a love that expands on the trails treaded by others.

The earth is a volcano of hatreds, crime akin to a lethal gas that poisons or deranges.

War is a cruel hydra always around.

"To live for oneself only" is a selfish philosophy of easy spread.

Only mercy redeems the criminal, reeducation preparing him or her for the trials of life.

Mercy is the antidote to hatred, the voice of reason overcoming instinct.

The mercy of the Father concedes the opportunity of rebirth in the stronghold of crime for the rehabilitation of the reprobate.

Forgiveness – an ennobling act, a non-transferable currency for spiritual growth.

Mercy – a love that succors and assists tirelessly.

"They shall obtain mercy!"

* * *

Truth comes forth in a new way.

It is not a litany.

The ode reaches its climax.

Jesus proclaims, with eloquent joy:

"Blessed are the pure in heart, for they shall see God!"

A state of near ecstasy sets in.

A delirium stirs the formerly amorphous and disconnected masses.

Tears can no longer be contained.

To cleanse the heart, the seat of feelings, in order to see God.

Under the burden of iniquity, hope is shattered.

Wallowing in filth, the pristine origins of love convert into a pestilential whirlpool.

To open the *eyes* of sentiment to see what reason dreams about and does not reach.

To be innocent and tune in with the Truth without rhetoric, harmony without disruption, so as to fulfill life and enjoy the vision of God.

As the Unattainable Transcendence, trying to humanize God to be registered by the human eye would be to trample on the aspiration of perfect identity with Him, the universally Immanent and invisible everywhere…

Uncaused Cause, one cannot condense Him in the luminous ray that produces the illusionary image presented by atoms.

Because the finite has wished to retain the Infinite, this finite has perverted and maculated the heart...

But to love the green grass, humankind, the sky, the animals, the insects, life in all its manifestations, to integrate oneself in the essence of the divine substance, hearts open to love, purity in everything.

"They shall see God!"

* * *

And the Master goes on, as if to complete the majestic teaching before incomprehension lays waste:

"Blessed are the peacemakers, for they shall be called children of God!"

To spread peace when the overall thought is to disrupt serenity.

The children of God shall inherit the earth because, being humble and meek, they shall be gentle of heart.

Gentleness, which is the courage to face the powerful without fearing them, to acquiesce without yielding to the dominance of force, to control anger and overcome oneself to pacify.

How many times had the Master applied unlimited energy in the face of hypocrisy and evil, maintaining austerity without violence, firmness of action without a hint of hatred, vigor without harshness, moral fortitude without emotional perturbation!

To expound without imposing.

To clear minds without bribing or subduing them, to lead without enslaving.

All human beings are in need of gentleness, they love and they need love, they identify and don't reject goodness, they recognize and are avid for pacification.

The mighty pass, the shadows of time engulfing them.

The peace we offer to others shall stay with them and with us, the gentleness with which we receive them, the benevolence extended to them, even though they might trample and harm us...

"They shall inherit the earth," the "children of God"!

* * *

And in the fraction of a minute, eternity beyond time, infinite beyond space, Jesus concludes tenderly:

"Blessed are those who endure persecution for the sake of justice, for theirs is the kingdom of heaven!"

Bliss is not a gratuitous bequest, insofar as peace is not a vain ornament.

Suffering deriving from persecution is a gift that enriches a spirit with peace, giving rise to bliss.

Persecutors are regrettable agents of misery.

In their sickness, they turn into criminals.

Deranged, they recruit followers of the same primitiveness they hide under, and under which they attack.

In all times honor suffers calumny and endures ridicule vitriol.

The heroes of the Truth silence the suffering of their hurting bodies, while the racket roars in deafening scorn.

Justice has its martyrs who fecund the arid soil for the coming of the Truth.

"For theirs is the kingdom of heaven!" For those who, blameless, suffered for their fidelity to Divine Justice.

* * *

The mantle of solar light crowns the peaks of the mountains beyond, exuberant at sunset.

In the wide meadow below, light dances between the shadows of the trees, while dusk reflects the glorious festival of the approaching nightfall.

Breathing is halted in all chests by silent cries, uneven heart palpitations freezing tense bodies.

He seems to caress the multitude, and with arms stretched out and hands like wings of light ready to soar, He says:

"Blessed are you when they have slandered you, and persecuted you, and spoken all kinds of evil against you, falsely, for my sake: be glad and exult, for your reward in heaven is plentiful. For so they persecuted the prophets who were before you!"

Sacrifice as the crowning of faith, a testimonial to belief.

Giving others the right to err, but not allowing oneself to commit wrongs.

To be pure without displays of external purity.

Aggressors persecuting with falsehoods; the assaulted remaining serenely unbroken.

The mud of smear does not stain immaculate purity.

Hands untainted by crimes; pure heart; righteous spirit.

The forbearers of the truth are so riveted in spreading this true ideal they don't have the time for lassitude or schemes. They even forget to defend their honor.

They don't remember to justify their acts, mocked by human sarcastic conveniences.

They are in the service of the Cause of Christ, expanding the immeasurable magnitude of love. Their self-denial and conduct speak higher than their words.

Their honor: the labor itself; their defense and argumentation: silence. The same response of those who were "persecuted before"...

They rejoice in righteousness, doing what they ought to do and not what is only convenient for them.

The glory of the fighters is the honor of service, their halo the sweat of duty.

"Rejoice and be glad!"

There are no longer doubts at this time.

The whole epic of Humanity is sung in the Sermon of the Mount.

Love in its highest expression finds in it its inexhaustible and eternal source.

* * *

The air is filled with the fragrances of Nature, the afternoon wind whooshes poetically.

The pause widens...

Emotions explode in bursts of peace and hope.

And He continues...

New hyperboles and hypallages express the blazing prelude of Truth like a thousand voices in harmony in a single voice never heard before...

". . . You are the salt of the earth..."

"You are the light of the world..."

"I did not come to destroy the law..."

"First go and be reconciled with your brother..."

"You shall not commit adultery, do not bring scandal..."

"Do not swear..."

"Do not resist an evil person..."

"Love your neighbor, love your enemies..."

"Be perfect..."

"Pray: Father Thou art in heaven..."

"Do not choose to store up for yourselves treasures on earth..."

The sun glows in the golden sunset.

Myriads of songs fill the air in the symphony of the twilight.

Huddling together, some in the multitude seemed to find solace in each other's weaknesses, in a gesture of union and identity.

The poem proceeds eloquently.

There is no time to waste.

". . . No one is able to serve two masters..."

"Consider the lilies of the field and the birds in the air..."

"Seek first the Kingdom of heaven and its Justice..."

"Do not judge..."

"Ask and you shall receive..."

"Seek and you shall find..."

"Knock and the door shall be opened..."

"Strive to enter through the narrow gate..."

"Beware of false prophets..."

The infinite sky becomes embroidered with stars.

The sunset glistens.

A great silence sets over the mountain.

Uplifted, the multitudes start to disperse.

Hearts are filled with joy and pain... Minds are burning with a strange fever.

The future awaits them.

Not far from now, as the legitimate heirs to the Kingdom of Heaven, these listeners will be invited for their testimony in prisons and at the stakes of martyrdom, among beasts and the battlefields of the world, in the crushing grips of severe afflictions.

Before the eyes of the Rabbi appear the scenes of the bloody struggles of the centuries to come for the implementation of those teachings in the world.

Jesus then descends the mountain and leaves, while some whisper about His authority.

It is almost night time.

The stars twinkle expressively as ever present silent witnesses.

* * *

The Magna Carta had been presented. The Good Tidings had been sung for the centuries to come.

The Sermon of the Mount is the alpha and the omega of the Doctrine of Jesus.

No Christian can cultivate evil due to ignorance.

It will never be repeated.

The wondrous event will be remembered forever.

History will conclude the song in the confines of eternity, in the future reencounter of the redeemed humanity with the Son of Man, the Redeemer.

CHAPTER 4

NICODEMUS, THE FRIEND

The full moon clothed Jerusalem in a silvery light.[20]

The tower of Antonia, rising high next to the Temple, is a sentinel of stone erected in the city of the prophets, watching for suspicious activities everywhere...

Outside the surrounding walls, the lush green slopes of Acra and Bezetha carried the cold wind in the direction of the sleeping city.

In the empty Temple, at that time of night, the fires of the eternal flame are crackling.

Nocturnal passersby carry torches despite the moonlight that is cast over the basalt floor.

The houses, their doors closed, lay immersed in profound silence.

Jesus, at the house of friends, waits.

Without any impediment, He had gladly agreed to that meeting. As if desiring it, soon after the request He generously acquiesced to it.

During those days in Jerusalem, He prepared the treats for the banquet of the anticipated day He so frequently mentioned.

---

[20] Jn. 3:1-15 (April 29 AD) – Spirit Auth.

Earlier He had been at the Temple disgracefully converted into a lair of greed.

He had taken vigorous action, while the money changers and merchants sprung to their feet, outraged… outraged by the Truth.

* * *

The Doctors of the Law were seventy in total, chosen in Israel among the well-educated and the nobility.

Nicodemus[21] was one of the youngest among the respectable scholars who had the privilege of occupying the high court of the Sanhedrin. A Pharisee, in addition to being a Doctor of the Law, he was also a ruler of the Jews.

Thirsting for the truth, he was not satisfied with the old forms of religious exegesis. He felt that, after the tortuous centuries during which Israel had been precluded from heavenly revelations, something strange and grand was in the air.

Of a noble character, he was austere in the interpretation of the Law and a zealous law-abiding individual.

He felt an unrestrained eagerness for renewal hovering around everywhere.

Rumors sprouted, some exaggerated others viable, of new prophets invigorating the unhappy masses with courage, consolation and hope.

He had heard of John, the itinerant preacher from the Jordan valley, but had feared to meet him.

He knew that John's fervent and passionate preaching could place him in a bad position before his peers in Jerusalem.

---

[21] Meaning of the name: "Victory of the People." – Spirit Auth.

The city was a den of spies, something that deeply anguished him.

Annas and Caiaphas, respectively father-in-law and son-in-law, fought almost openly for the supremacy at the Sanhedrin, the webs of intrigue casting their traps everywhere. Herod had recruited militiamen who blended with the populace, hidden in every corner, while Rome kept a dominant watch…

He wished for the truth, but not to the extent of compromising his position.

He knew of Jesus.

The Messiah, of Whom he would hear through others, seemed to attract him vigorously.

He had had contact with many of those who knew Him and had been succored by Him.

He had been informed of the new and invigorating content of His speeches.

For a long time now he had been waiting for someone who would show the evident signs of courage and equilibrium, fearlessness and discernment as an excelling son of God, to steer the suffering people of Israel. Someone who would enlighten the minds constricted by the rigors of the applications of the Law or deceived by the usurpation of the wealth of the widows and orphans, exchanged for false prayers in criminal schemes.

Jesus was now in Jerusalem.

Jesus would see him; and he, Nicodemus, would hear Him.

The meeting was set for late night. It would be more discreet.

A friend of his would take him to the house of another mutual friend where He, Jesus, would be staying overnight, in the Valley of Cedron, beyond the city walls…

* * *

Taken there by one of His devoted disciples, once Nicodemus got to the house and saw Him, he could not contain the sudden emotion that struck him.

He had the impression of knowing Him.

Jesus also seemed to cordially recognize him, as if He already knew him and was waiting for this meeting.

In a split second he tried to remember, *in his heart,* where he had seen Him before, but to no avail.

In the acoustics of the mind he seemed to hear Him say: "I know you, Nicodemus ben Gurion, from before…"

Controlling his emotions, he quickly composed himself for the ensuing dialogue.

* * *

The large terrace with its colored latticework offered a view of the walls of the sleeping Jerusalem.

The dreamy and starry night covered the breezy rolling hills in a silvery light.

The room, illuminated by a sizzling oil lamp, sheltered the two guests, silently facing each other.

Nicodemus' anticipation was immeasurable. A passionate spirit, he knew the worldly glories and had drenched himself in flattery. He represented the restless, the unstable, the anxious humankind.

Jesus personified peace. Serene, He observed the man who had come to question Him.

Two very distinct worlds…

No longer able to contain his racing emotions, the Doctor of the Law asked Him:

"Rabbi, we know that you are a teacher come from God, for no one can do these signs that you do unless God is with him."

The Master's face, crowned by wavy hair falling to his shoulders, seemed to be transfigured. His eyes shone with a strange and translucent light.

"What do you want from me?" asked Jesus.

"What does one need to do," answered the Pharisee emotively "to enjoy the pinnacles of peace with a righteous mind and a serene heart?... And after that enjoy the delights of the Kingdom?"

For how long had that question burned in his mind?

He wished for that answer but feared finding it.

He wished to know the truth but was fearful of it.

The truth had been the reason for his unceasing search, but at the same time he was aware that to know it would be to die to all illusions, to bear the oppressing burden of incomprehension and struggles with a firm spirit after this knowledge.

In the Master's presence and infused by His magnetism, Nicodemus felt this to be the decisive moment of his whole existence.

He waited for the response, after which he would start to live, dying to everything he had amassed so far in life...

The questions hovered in the room.

Observing that man of noble spirit so lost in the labyrinths of conventions, suffocated by deceitful external practices, the Rabbi replied:

"Truly, truly, I say to you, unless one has been born again by water and the Holy Spirit, he is not able to enter into the kingdom of God ..."

The answer was complex and profound.

What could it be "to be born again," pondered Nicodemus, and without hesitation he asked further:

"How could a man be born when he is old? Surely, he cannot enter a second time into his mother's womb to be born again?"

The Master gazed at him for a while.

Nicodemus felt embarrassed.

"When I speak of 'being born again'," continued the Rabbi, "I want to convey the necessity of being born of water and the spirit. What is born of the flesh is flesh, and what is born of the Spirit is spirit. You should not be amazed that I said to you: You must be born anew. The Spirit inspires where he wills. And you hear his voice, but you do not know where he comes from, or where he is going. So it is with all who are born of the Spirit."

Such strange answer.

Nicodemus considers: were the Essenes knowledgeable after all about the kingdom of God? Like the Ancients and the Tradition, they also talked about rebirths.

He knew that in the Egyptian Mysteries, along with the metempsychosis with which the wretched were threatened, the priests also talked to the initiates about the many Incarnations of the Spirit in order to rid itself from wrongdoings and imperfections. Could 'to be born again' be similar to the doctrine of successive lives mentioned by the Hindus and the Greeks?

The need to be reborn seemed logical to him. To *repay* in a *lifetime* the *debts* incurred in *another*. To redo the pathway already treaded, rectifying errors and smoothing out edges.

However, there was no time to be lost in ponderings.

As if waking up to this teaching, the Doctor of the Law sought further confirmation:

"How can this be?"

"You are a teacher in Israel," answered Jesus, "and you do not understand these things? All those who study the old scrolls know the pathway of evolution. 'We speak of what we know, and we testify to what we have seen, but still you people do not accept our testimony.' These are the teachings on the earthly level. I could speak of heavenly things, but you would not understand them. The spirit is imperishable and in its infinite journey it pauses to reflect and recommence to ascend further. The neglected or too complex commitments of today will be rectified tomorrow…"

Emotion vibrated on the lips of the Rabbi.

It was almost a monologue.

Perhaps at that moment He was addressing all Humankind.

Wishing to imprint upon the perplexed and spellbound visitor these secure guidelines, in addition to identifying Himself as the One sent by God, He continued:

"And no one (from the Earth) has ascended to heaven, except the one who descended from heaven: the Son of man who is in heaven. And just as Moses lifted up the serpent in the desert, so also must the Son of Man be lifted up, so that whoever believes in Him may not perish, but may have eternal life…"

What did He mean by "the serpent"? Salomon referred to it as a symbol of sacrifice, thought Nicodemus.

Would it be necessary for the Rabbi to be sacrificed in order for the truth to be spread in the hearts and for humankind to identify the truth? Nicodemus felt that he already loved Him in his heart and a silent worry entered his mind.

Nicodemus' eyes were moist with tears.

The Rabbi stood up.

The ample room felt silent.

The stars blinked far away.

The visit had come to an end.

Nicodemus gazed at the Master bathed in light. He bid Him farewell and, wrapped in his mantle, disappeared into the night in the direction of Jerusalem.

The truth would continue to open new paths in the minds and would guide the spirits.

The Doctrine of Successive Lives had been taught by Jesus. Reincarnation would decipher the enigmas of life in the future to come.

* * *

John, very moved with the revelatory dialogue, continued in conversation with the Master on that sublime night and later would write about the coming of the Son of Man. Perhaps appreciative to Nicodemus, whom he did not forget, John will refer to him after the sacrifice on the cross ...

The Gospel did announce the excellence of the revelation in the dialogue with Nicodemus, the man who had sought out Jesus. There were no more doubts.

On the dark dome of the sky the sparkling stars, on the gloomy earth the One who is the "Light of the World" shining the truth into the hearts.

CHAPTER 5

THE RICH YOUNG MAN

The moment had a profound meaning. Through a strange intuition he knew that one day he would be confronting Reality, and he was facing it now.[22]

In the afternoon stifling air, Nature stood still.

Sweet fragrances drifted from small flowers spread over the edges of the slope. Transparent waters sung unknown melodies, flowing over a bed of rounded rocks.

The appeal lingered, resonating all around: "If you are willing to be perfect, go, sell what you have, and give to the poor, and then you will have treasure in heaven. And then come, and follow me."

That voice pierced like a sharp dagger and permeated like a lemongrass scent.

The unmistakable magnetism emitted by those austere and deep eyes resembling two stars embedded in the pale face of dawn.

He was thirsting for peace.

Although he slept on a bed of precious woods inlaid with ebony and lapis-lazuli, feasted on sumptuous meals, had

---

22 Mt. 19:16-30; Mk. 10:17-31; Lk. 18:18-30. – Spirit Auth.

his body massaged with rare oils and ointments and covered in fabrics of light linen, had trunks spilling over with gems and gold, he felt melancholy, he knew he was not happy. Something not easily obtained was missing.

Nonetheless, he wavered.

His villa was luxurious, his possessions magnificent, but his heart was empty.

While youth was all about happiness, parties and constant invitations to delight his agile and vigorous body, he yearned for higher aspirations, for the total attainment of peace. This need was more than a torment. He did not wish for the ostentatious tranquility of the Pharisees or the numbing repose of the opulent merchants, nor the deceitful serenity of the rich money changers or the victorious decrepitude of the conquerors in compulsory retirement. He was searching for a harmonious integration into something, but he did not how what it was.

Afflicted and distraught, he was unaware of the causes of this persistent melancholy, a sadness that dissolved his dreams and hopes under the grip of an indescribable agony.

He sought out competitions in Caesarea, but did not know if this pursuit meant an accomplishment or an escape.

Now, for the first time, he felt enraptured.

The gentleness and command of that voice, emanating from that Man, echoed like chaotic cascades in the abysses of his spirit.

Inwardly he was shouting "I will go with you, Lord, but…"

He was still hesitant and the hour did not allow for any doubt.

Red flowers of a rosebush hugging the branches of nearby shrubbery were suddenly shaken by the wind, and on the terrace petals the color of blood fell as omens at his feet …

From where did he know Him? He pondered apprehensively, trying hard to remember.

Everything in that hour was important – more than that, it was vital!

Seeing Him from afar, it felt like reencountering a friend, a Celestial Friend.

When his eyes met with His gaze he felt naked, his heart pounding violently. Unusual emotions vibrated in his whole being like never before. He wanted to drop to the ground, an incontrollable chest tightness crushing him.

He saw the Stranger smiling, as if waiting for him, as if He loved him – he was certain of that.

Time was racing by, rushing its fleeting hours.

His lips seemed to be sealed, an impertinent coldness freezing his hands.

He was struggling to break the numbness paralyzing him.

Patches of moonlight timidly shone on the loose clouds in the firmament, embroidering with light the haughty olive trees and oleanders in bloom.

"Let me," he was able to say overcoming the emotion that transfigured him, "let me first compete in the games in Caesarea to win the prizes for Israel …"

"I cannot wait. The Kingdom of Heaven starts today and now for your spirit. There is no time to lose."

"But I have waited for so long for this event, and it is now so close with the start of the racing season… I have trained so hard, I hired slaves to coach me… I spent a fortune buying two pairs of fiery horses from the Parthians… the games will be so soon…"

"Renounce everything, come, and follow me!"

Who was this Man who spoke to him in such a way? What power did He exert over his will? By what sortilege did

He dominate him? … He wanted to flee, he wanted to stay; he felt utterly distressed, an unknown turmoil pounding him…

The horizontality of human afflictions encountering the verticality of divine sublimation; the mundane facing the infinite; the valley gazing at the heights, lost in that immensity.

Man and the Son of Man face to face.

The dialogue seemed impossible, reduced to a tortured monologue for the young man in the presence of that Man.

Fighting an overwhelming fear, the rich prince continued:

"I can give everything I have: money, gold, jewels, titles if necessary, that would be easy, but…"

"… Give me of yourself and I will offer you everlasting bliss."

What a high reward! And what a high price! He concluded, discouraged.

He was very young and trusted by so many. Israel would possibly profit from his laurels and triumphs. A prince, he had before him the paths of power to which he clung, but a power that at that moment was far from any value.

His possessions he could indeed give away. But the riches of youth, the vibrant treasures of vanities and fancies, the family honors upheld in traditions, the pleasing admirers and flatterers, would it be necessary to renounce to all this? These restless thoughts kept flooding his mind.

"Yes!" Was the silent reply of those resplendent eyes.

In those brief moments the young man suffered all the torments of his life at once.

The air whispered softly while fragrant wild tulips wove a gentle mantle over the fields.

The Rabbi waited in silence. The young man still perplexed, lost in inner upheaval.

The dialogue was no longer possible.

Suddenly, in a split second, the talented prince remembered friends waiting for him in the city. Pressing engagements requiring his attention. He needed to discuss the final details of next week's big race.

Driven by a strange abrupt impulse, he turned to the serene and sorrowful Messiah and whispered in a low voice:

"I can't... I can't follow you now... Forgive me if you love me!

And he left almost running.

* * *

Cold winds blew from afar, set to music by the flickering of the twinkling stars.

The earth glowing under dew-covered grass.

The Master sat down, filled with deep sadness.

He always felt that way after the desertion of those invited for the Banquet of Light. The gentle and forgiving expression shining in his eyes would fill with tears, enveloped in light traces of sorrow.

To the disciples who found Him this way, He responded:

"How difficult it will be for those who have riches to enter the Kingdom of God!"

* * *

One week later Caesarea was the capital of leisure and pleasure.

Located north to the Plain of Sharon and 30 kilometers[23] south of Mt. Carmel, Caesarea had been beautified by Herod.

---

[23] App. 18.6 miles. – Tr.

He had ordered the construction of a large sea port, known for its colossal pier, and had embellished the city with an imposing Temple where a monumental statue of the Emperor had been erected.

This valuable port on the Mediterranean was an important outlet for Israel, a maritime gateway where vessels from everywhere would be docked.

Villas with their gardens leaned over the city's brownish slopes, exhibiting their various architectural styles.

Its amenable climate turned it into the official residence of the Roman procurators in Israel.

Tamarinds oscillating in the wind adorned the streets while exotic aromas blended in the atmosphere swept by the sea air.

Scarlet anemones[24] or "lilies of the field" and white narcissus or "roses of Sharon" mingled in the plains.

The festivals of Caesarea intended to rival with those of Rome, attracting aficionados from as far as the metropolis itself.

The public festivities started with the joyful sound of horns and fanfares.

Chariot competitions opened the races under the nervousness of Jews, Romans, and Gentiles who placed high bets on their aces on the gambling tables.

Gladiators in simulated combats, flute, lute, and cymbals players fill the intervals between the races with sound and color.

---

[24] In his Sermon on the Mount, Jesus mentioned "lilies of the field." Tulips, poppies, daisies and other wildflowers have been suggested as candidates for "lilies of the field. . . . Crown Anemone, also known as Windflower, grows abundantly in hills, valleys and fields throughout Israel. Its six to nine velvety petals are usually a <u>deep red</u>, but there are also white, pink and lavender varieties. This anemone has been more recently "traditionally" regarded as the lily of the field. (Emphasis added.) http://www.jerusalemperspective.com. – Tr.

The *quadrigae* are positioned at the starting line. Shiny and bejeweled spirited horses, bought from the Parthians from Dalmatia, Tyro, Sidon, and Arabia, strut vigorously. At the signal, they bolt off under a thunderous ovation.

Whips lashing in the air, hands tight on the reigns, charioteers speed up their fragile vehicles. The celerity makes everyone hold their breath.

Expectations erupt without a voice in the pulsating hot and dusty afternoon.

During a less fortunate maneuver a chariot flips over, a body falls in the arena, fast racing hooves tearing it apart.

Breathing stertorously, the young rich man feels his open wounds, sweat and blood soaking the mud...

As quick slaves pull him from the track he mentally flees the brutal scene crushing him, and through the fog that falls over his eyes he seems to see Him again.

Silencing the screams in the acoustic shell, he has the impression of hearing Him:

""Renounce everything, come, and follow me!"

"Dear friend! ..."

Two transparent and gentle arms embrace him.

Despite his disfigured face, awash in tears, sweat and blood, he gives the impression of smiling.

SEED OF LIGHT AND LIFE

It was a sunny morning.[25]

Clouds drifted on the fringes of the diurnal wind.

The immense multitudes on the ground, farther than the eye could see.

The considerable extension of the land waiting to be tilled by the promising plow.

The sea, this old friend, rolling its white foam-crowned waves towards the sand and pebbles of the broad beach.

Sitting in the boat, Jesus lengthened His gaze over the grounds, the multitude of hearts, and thought of the untilled land. Filled with great love for humankind, after speaking of many things, He continued:

"*Behold, a sower went out to sow seed. And while he was sowing, some fell beside the road.*"

Light pours streaks of living gold in the blue sky.

The transparent air caresses the rapt ears of the multitude.

"*... And the birds of the air came and ate it...*"

The kingdom of God is similar...

---

[25] Mt. 13:1-23; Mk. 11:1-20; Lk. 8:4-15. – Spirit Auth.

A god man sowed a good seed in good soil; while he slept a wretched man threw weed seeds in the same good soil. In order to save the good seed it was necessary to pull up the weeds, which also dug up many of the good seeds. The weeds in bundles were burned while the bagged wheat was stored in the granary.

* * *

A grain of mustard is the smallest of all, but it grows into a big tree. Many birds seek shelter in its branches...

* * *

The insignificant yeast makes the whole dough rise...

* * *

A man found a treasure so valuable that he sold everything he had to own it.

Another man discovered a pearl of incomparable value and left everything behind to possess it...

* * *

A net cast into the sea caught many fish, good and bad, which were separated by the fisherman. Likewise, human beings that aspire to the kingdom of heaven will be separated ...

* * *

"Then others fell in a rocky place, where they did not have much soil. But when the sun rose up, they were scorched, and because they had no roots, they withered ..."

What is hidden He reveals in parables.

Once upon a time...

A man, the head of a household, prepared the soil, planted it, enclosed it with a trench, built a wine press on it, erected a tower, and then leased it to other workers. At the time of the harvest he sent for the part that was due to him. Squatters on the land killed the first servants, then those who came after that, and even the *son of man* was killed by the villains. However, when the owner returned...

* * *

The father said to the son: Come to work in my vineyard.

"I don't want to!" But having repented, he went. When the second son was called, he replied:

"I'll go!" But he did not follow through...

* * *

The king, at the time of the wedding of his son, sent his servants to invite his friends. These friends, however, did not want to go. Other servants went out and repeated the invitation, describing the excellence of the banquet waiting for them, but they did not want to savor it. Bothered by the insistence of the king, they killed the servants. The king, aware of the ingratitude of the invitees, ordered his army to exterminate the murderers...

* * *

They were ten in all.

Five were foolish brides. They wasted the oil and were left without light. They went to sleep. When the grooms arrived…

They were five foolish brides…

* * *

"I knew you are severe. Afraid, I buried the talent you entrusted to me."

"You wicked, lazy servant! Take the talent from him and give it to the one with ten."

* * *

Melodies sing in the light and transparent air.

"…*Still others fell among thorns, and the thorns increased and suffocated them* …"

Who puts a lamp under a bushel or keeps it hidden?

* * *

The fig tree by the road was requested to bear fruit. As it was not the right season to produce them, it was considered disgraced, fit to be pulled out and thrown into the fire until it turned into ashes…

* * *

The Doctor of the Law replied emphatically: "The one who showed mercy to him."

Go and do the same. This is your neighbor…

* * *

Friend, can I have three loaves of bread…
"Don't bother me."
And to rid himself from the annoyance, the friend who was asked will walk away…

* * *

Oh! Tell my brother to divide the inheritance with me.
"Who appointed me to be a judge or arbitrator over you people?"

* * *

Do not take the place of honor without having been assigned to it by your host…

* * *

"…*Yet some others fell upon good soil, and they produced fruit: some one hundred fold, some sixty fold, some thirty fold. …*"
Hyperbaton, synchysis, and hyperbole clothe abstractions, and like small poems are snippets of life singing the songs of the kingdom of God.
Once upon a time…
There was a certain moneylender that had two debtors and since none could pay him back…
Blessed are those servants, whom the Lord will find watching when He comes…

* * *

"Whoever who does not take up their cross and follow me…"

"Father, I have sinned against heaven and before you. Now I am not worthy to be called your son."

"Quickly! Bring out the best robe, and clothe him with it. And put a ring on his hand and shoes on his feet. For this son of mine was dead, and has revived; he was lost, and is found…"

* * *

The Pharisee prayed: I pay tithes, I perform the duties prescribed by the Law… I'm certainly not like the other one over there…

However, the Lord said to him…

* * *

And the lord praised the iniquitous steward, in that he had acted prudently. For the sons of this world are more prudent with their generation than the sons of light… Make friends… Whoever is faithful in what is least is also faithful in what is greater …

* * *

And the widow said: Vindicate me from my adversary…

I will vindicate her, said the judge, so that she no longer pesters me…

* * *

"He gave them ten minas…"

"There was a rich man, to whom after his death Father Abraham said…"

"The last shall be the first, and the first last…"

"Whoever has ears, let them hear…"

* * *

He spoke through parables.

Parables are "allegories that illustrate hidden truths."

Imbued with the purity of doves and the prudence of serpents the disciples of truth will come to be.

"If you have faith the size of a mustard seed…"

Parables, truths in allegories.

* * *

The seeds turn into grains, and the blessed harvest is gold in the streams of life.

Simple and unadorned, His words are the same words spoken by the people. But no one ever put them together as He did when He spoke them.

There was "something" in Him, in His way of saying them.

No one speaks as He speaks – whispered even those who, conspiring against Him, sought ways to betray Him.

He speaks with authority – and everybody recognized it.

* * *

A seed is light and life.

Life in the seed.

Light in life.

* * *

The Good Shepherd gives His Life for his sheep.

Entering through the narrow door, the one marked by the difficulties, the access to the kingdom of complete Bliss is triumphant.

Watching at the entrance door, the dweller can defend the house against the robbers who lurk outside dressed like shadows to strike in the shadows…

The chosen are the blissful seeds that multiply into a thousand other seeds, boosting the entire sowing.

* * *

The arid and uncultivated land of passions is a field of hope under the action of the seed.

In the vast plains, however, humankind's daily lives become fruitless exertions.

The soil to be tilled, immense, almost abandoned…

"The sower went to sow."

* * *

Parables and the spirit of life.

Life in the parables.

To His inner circle, to the disciples, He explained them.

* * *

It is no longer daylight.

The black mantle of the night flickers in the shining settings of the stars while the wind sings an onomatopoeic uninterrupted litany.

The sower rests.

"The kingdom of heaven lies within you…"

"You are gods…"

"First seek the kingdom…"

"And when I have been lifted up from the earth, I will draw all things to myself."

* * *

The dawn of the New Era is near..

The sower was lifted … on a cross.

Wounded, the arms drawing near, the heart awaits.

Pathway to Life – the sower.

Pathway to the door – the sower.

The cross of renunciation and sacrifice akin to a harsh plough in the field of the spirit – a bridge between the abysses: the "I" close by and "Him" so close and yet so far.

The arid and uncultivated land displays the star.

The star descends to the mire, gets caught in the water that retains it, and rests on the soaring mountain.

* * *

The sower waits…

"He went to teach by parables."

"*Yet some others fell upon good soil, and they produced fruit.*"

The seed is the Word for those who search for the Truth.

Truth is Life.

The sower went to sow…

THE PARALYTIC OF CAPERNAUM

The small town lay asleep on the northern side of Lake Gennesaret. All around, hills covered with green olive groves and lush vineyards tilting over higher elevations and bare cliffs with their protruding boulders. The valleys were cooler, crisscrossed by singing creeks and crystal-clear small waterfalls.[26]

The lake's shores and fish-abundant waters were much sought after by fishermen. Fishing nets dangled in the sun, casting shadows on pebbles chiseled by lapping waves, while old fig trees and tamarinds spread their branches in the swaying breezes.

Capernaum was a poem of tenderness with its low houses spread out among leafy trees, inlaid with small colored climbing flowers.

He loved that city and had chosen it to start His ministry of love.

The month of May unleashed the scorching rays of the sun; devoid of the undulating sways brought by the wind the trees seemed made out of stone.

---

[26] Mt. 9:1-8; Mk. 2:1-12; Lk. 5:17-26. – Spirit Auth.

Since the day before the news had traveled by word-of-mouth, attracting the curious and the afflicted of the surrounding regions.

Although He had imposed silence to the leper He had cured, and had requested Simon Peter's mother-in-law not to speak of *what happened to her*, to keep the events quiet was almost impossible.

Need and suffering in their gloom look for the faintest sparks of hope and impel the afflicted souls in that direction.

He gave His tender love to these shoreline communities, and the simple and trusting hearts of the people loved Him back.

The moment had come for the Shepherd to rise to lead the immense flock, across rough tracts of land, harsh paths, crossing abysses.

This was the prelude to the Message and the beginning of His suffering...

* * *

The activities were varied and feverish.

The complaints and sufferings of the multitude filled the air with afflictive miasmas. Despite the number of those healed, after they joyfully announced their recovery new droves in disarray would soon follow, peddling their miseries.

The serene face of the Rabbi contracted in the heavy, stifling air of the room without ventilation. The never-ending tumult, the appeals and imprecations multiplying in all voices...

Standing at the door, Simon Peter showed indescribable happiness. To the back of the house – its yard stretching all the way to the shoreline – was the sea Simon loved so much. At the front, amid the crowd, the Master curing and consoling the afflicted of this world as an Ambassador of Heaven. Inwardly he thanked God that his house had been chosen, and that he had been called to His flock. Simon did not notice the hours flying by. Emotions were so many and so hard to explain that he just quietly observed the flow of pain and joy before him: grimaces transformed into smiles, tears into praises, festering sores into cleansed tissue... all accomplished by His laying-on-of-hands, the vibration of His voice, or the light of His eyes...

Never before in Israel had something similar ever happened. Unclean spirits would flee, and pain and suffering would loosen their grip at the command of His voice...

Simon's sparkling eyes met His gaze. For a moment he had the impression that He was asking for his help. His features seemed transparent, exhaustion stamped in His sweaty and sorrowful face...

The humble fisherman understood: the multitudes were insatiable, suffering had no limit; it was imperative to help Him by removing Him from there.

He broke through the crowd, announcing loudly:

"The Master is tired!"

Simon tenderly takes Him by the arm and gently walks Him to the beach.

Stars began to sparkle in the sky as the sun sets in the horizon, leaving a streak of glowing gold beyond the mountains on the other side of the lake.

Gusts of warm wind arrive on the crest of the waves, white laces of foam breaking onto the shores thirsty for the caresses of the waters.

The Rabbi sat on the high roots of an old tree spreading its branches towards the lake, and in silence entered into deep meditation.

Simon, as a faithful friend, sat next to Him, gazing at His pale and exhausted face.

The wavy hair the color of amber, fluttering in disarray amid the gusts of wind, His eyes profound and mysterious as the depth of the lake that Simon had known all his life.

How handsome was the Rabbi! – thought Simon – a handsomeness he had never seen before. There was *something* in Him that made Him different from all other people. Slender and well built, not especially an athlete, neither thin nor feeble, a powerful force with an unusual majesty. Simple and kind, He was wise and humble. Deeply knowledgeable about human misery, He sought out the suffering and the afflicted to alleviate them. He spoke little but said much, with words everybody spoke, but no one else spoke like He did. However, in that humble and pure Man, bearer of unusual beauty of body and spirit, loomed tinges of a profound melancholy...

Simon entered into deep thought also.

Only the night itself broke the silence, following the voices of Nature.

Suddenly, as if coming from far away, Simon looked at Him again and only then he was able to see it. The large and clear eyes of the Rabbi were immersed in tears...

His heart beating wildly in his inner distress, Simon asked anxiously:

"Rabbi, are you crying?"

"..."

"... I suppose of happiness, considering the happy events of the day, right?"

The question hovered in the nightly air.

The old tree shook its branches, the voice of the lake singing a special plainchant, its panting waves breaking on its vast shores.

"Yes, Simon, I'm weeping," He replied slowly. "I weep with sorrow, with compassion."

"But, Master, I do not understand. Today you bared yourself to the cunning and insolent Pharisees, to the ambitious and deceitful Scribes who came to spy, to the mob of traitors, and for all to see you forgave sins and healed, silencing them with wisdom and elevation ... and now you cry?"

"Yes, because I'm not understood by you and by them. I certainly don't expect to be understood. However, I have pity on them, those who lack discernment, and I lament them."

* * *

Nathaniel Ben Elijah, in an inn in the city, exulted in the company of jugs of rich wine and truculent friends.

"A miracle happened in my misery," he announced with alacrity.

"Tell us, tell us what happened because we doubt what we heard!" Many asked in one voice.

"It was so sudden that I'm still stunned," he replied.

"As you all know," he wiped away the sweat of his face altered by the emotion, "paralysis and fevers had plagued me for a while, tying me to a filthy and despicable cot, impeding me to move, turning me into a repulsive reprobate.

"Totally forgotten on my mat, until some hours ago I had been a victim of extreme physical and moral misery.

"I was waiting for death, which kept delaying itself, to free me.

"I had heard of Him and wept for the chance to meet Him. A secret intuition telling me that He would be able to cure me...

"Knowing that He was in Capernaum today, I asked some friends to take me to Him, and my friends, lifting the cot where I suffered my bitter misery, took me to the house where He was staying. The crowd was so thick they could not take me to the door.

"All around screams, desperation and altercations causing awful and deplorable scenes.

"Seeing the affliction and dismay in my gaunt face, one of my friends had the idea of lifting me to the upper terrace and to lower me through the ceiling down to His presence. And so it was done. Climbing the outside lateral stairs of fisherman Simon's house, they broke through the adobe and frantically tore the roof mats and palm branches between the ceiling beams until they got an opening large enough to pass my cot through the hole, tied to some cords.

"The crowded room opened a small space, as if He was waiting for me. He looked at me for a while, in silence, examining my physical ruin. And then He spoke:"

"Nathanael Ben Elijah, do you believe I can cure you?"

"The velvety voice was strong, gentle, yet firm.

"Yes", I replied, "I believe it!

"A tremor shook me. A great silence followed and even the heat seemed to abate.

"Lord!" I cried out. "How do you know my name? Do you know me?"

"Yes, I know you, Nathaniel, *since yesterday*. I am the Good Shepherd and because of it I know the names of all the sheep entrusted to me by my Father."

"I must confess I did not understand what He meant by *since yesterday*. I had never seen Him before, nor did He ever visit me…"

"Your sins," He said, "are forgiven!"

"Grumbles and angry reactions could be heard from the crowd. Even I became distressed.

"I cannot tell you how many times I thought of following a clean and decent life if I could walk again, move my limbs. However, right then I asked myself: was He really able to pardon any sins? Was He not blaspheming? Sweat was covering my scrawny and filthy body.

"As if He heard my most inner thoughts, without any reservations, He questioned:"

"Which is easier to say, 'Your sins are forgiven you' or to say 'Rise up and walk?'"

"And turning to me, He stretched out his arms and hands, commanding in a firm tone:"

"Rise, take up your mat, and walk."

"I shook like a reed in the wind, wanted to talk but could not.

"I picked up the mat, exploding in screams of happiness: 'Praise the Rabbi!' And I came back giving hosannas, for all those who knew me were quite surprised.

"I still don't know what happened to me, it seems like a dream from which I'm afraid to wake up."

"Let's drink to it!" shouted all those around him. "Let's drink to your recovered health ... and to pleasure! Show us your body without any marks or sores so we can believe it even more..."

Sensual music followed, flowing from the fingers of unfortunate women hired from Nubia and other lands for the commerce of the flesh as they played their string instruments and tambourines, filling the ample room saturated by exotic aromas.

Outside, the night peeked at the earth through the eyes of the stars.

* * *

"Why do You say that we don't understand You, Rabbi? We are all so happy!"

"Simon, at this very moment, while you consider the kingdom of heaven for what you have seen, Nathaniel, with childish delight, comments the event among drunken friends and unfortunate women. Others who regained their courage or recovered their voice are plunging themselves in the abysses of folly among exclamations of happiness, resulting in new unbalance – but this time irreversible.

"Do not believe that the Good Tidings shall bring superficial delights, the ones that disenchantment and suffering will easily erase."

"The Son of Man, therefore, is not an irresponsible mender, who sows new patches onto old and tattered fabric, damaging the torn part with a greater tear. It would be a disaster to store in old and filthy vessels the new and rich wine that would thus not ferment timely.

"The message of the Kingdom, more than a promise for the future is a reality for the present. It penetrates inwardly and dignifies, revealing life in amazing colors…

"However, I know that you and they cannot understand me for now. And thus it should be for some time to come.

"Later, after suffering has produced a greater maturity in the spirits, I will send Someone in my name to continue the service of illumination of consciences. The sepulchers will break their silence and Voices everywhere will proclaim, teaching hope under the auspices of a thousand consolations…"

The Master silenced for a while.

The sparkling eyes of the old fisherman expressed the emotions that sang in the core of his being.

The light air passed through the leaves of the trees while the high tide foretold a great pause in the pulsating nature.

"And when this Consoler arrives," interrupted the disciple very moved, "will humankind receive it with understanding?"

"No, Simon" replied Jesus. "Not in the beginning.

"The efficient methods for healing and discipline are severe, and for this reason undesired. However, this Envoy will stay indefinitely with Humanity, assisting without weariness and slowly constructing the untarnished Era of Peace and Happiness.

"It will remove old obstacles, it will promote social restructuring through love, which will penetrate all segments of life, launching sentiments of solidarity in all hearts..."

The face of the Master was transfigured.

Simon could not stop the free flowing of tears.

And the centuries continued to pass speedily through the hourglass of time...

THE PLEA OF THE CANAANITE WOMAN

Travelers crossing the Phoenician border in the direction of Tyre and Sidon would find themselves in the old domains of the Canaanites.[27]

In that territory lived the descendants of the Canaanites – also called Syrian-Phoenicians to distinguish them from the Phoenicians from Libya, since from the days of Pompey the Great Phoenicia had been annexed to Syria.

With the constant migrations brought by the conquerors since the times of the Macedonians, the Ptolomies, the Lagids, the Canaanite people intermingled with the invaders, enabling the proliferation of worship of the diverse deities that would mix with Moloch, Baal, Tanit ... together with the gods of Egypt and Hellas.

While in Judea Hellenization experienced the most vigorous rejection, thus preserving the country like an oasis in the worship of the "One God" only, in Phoenicia and Syria

---

[27]   Mt. 15:21-28; Mk. 7:24-30. – Spirit Auth.

miscegenation had extended toward religion, facilitating an unbridled path to orgiastic paganism.

At the time of the universalization of worship through an Imperial Roman decree, the Canaanites had perfectly assimilated the beliefs and taboos of those who had roamed their provinces.

The cities of Tyre and Sidon, towards which Jesus and the Twelve where heading, were famous for the manufacturing of luxury goods and well known by the legends that filled the Western mind with respect to the Far East.

Splendid and majestic pagan temples could be found amid fragrant groves, while beautiful constructions of inlaid marble stood out in the green grass scenery.

* * *

Tempers were flaring up in those days.

The straightforwardness of the Rabbi's vigorous speech did not allow for misinterpretation. His teachings were seeds of truth.

Probed, He would answer with lucid confidence. His concepts did not align with the strange practices in vogue, nor did they submit to the existing rules.

Giving those who followed Him a clear direction, His comments established the inevitable parallel between Pharisaism and the Gospel's Good Tidings.

Upright, He would never bow to flattery or despotism.

After facing with stoicism those who came from Jerusalem to interrogate Him, soon after He decided to travel to other parts.

Gathering the disciples, He headed northwest along the Jordan River as if searching for the river's sources…

It was not the first time he would meet with the Gentiles...

* * *

His name had already gone beyond the narrow limits of Galilee and many came to hear Him, informed by travelers and caravans that had crossed the distances.

Close by, the sea reflected the fiery skies of the sunset and the breezes ran fast teeming with exotic aromas.

The disciples, although silent, mentally asked themselves what objectives could there be to take them to those unrepentant *gentile* pagan cities.

The Great Hermon, the mountain range, the blessed lands had stayed behind...

The pagans' execrating worship exhaled turpitude. So, what were they doing in such a place?

Judaism was the revelation and the Master was the answer of God to the afflicted pleas of humankind, they knew it. Would it be righteous therefore to mix with these ungodly worshippers of idols?

After a while, walking part of the night, they finally reached Tyre. Crossing the city without any incident, they went in search of shelter.

The next day, before walking a furlong[28] beyond the city gates in the direction of Sidon, after seeing them passing by and then following them closely, a distressed voice spoke out loud:

"Take pity on me, Lord, Son of David! My daughter is badly afflicted by a demon."

---

[28]   220 yards (approximately 200 meters). – Tr.

Some of the disciples turned to look at the woman who so desperately pleaded for help.

They realized she was a foreigner ...

Even if she had been a descendant of Israel – given that she had identified Him as the "Son of David" – in those days she was professing an execrable and abject religion. They completely ignored her.

As her laments and pleas turned into frenetic agitation, some approached Him and suggested:

"Dismiss her, for she is crying out after us."

Picking up the pace, Jesus replied compassionately to the afflicted woman:

"I was not sent except to the lost sheep of Israel."

His voice was firm, but the words were uttered with gentleness and benevolence.

In a split second the woman mentally recalled her life. Her daughter was her treasure, a treasure she fought to preserve. Misfortune took everything she had along the years: happiness, husband, friends. She desperately struggled for a better future, and her daughter was at the center of it. She did not recall any offense against the Heavens.

Regaining her composure in her humble condition, and reconsidering her plea, she implored:

"Lord, help me!"

Suffering and intense trust were visible in her.

Jesus looked at her for a while, as if pondering what He would say to her.

He knew the excellence of the faith that pulsated in that heart. But He also knew the Israelite pride and disdain toward foreigners.

At other times, amid the loathed rabble or while succoring those outside of Israel's tutelage, He had been met with distrust and even disgust. However, He was now in the presence of someone harboring the precious gems of love and faith.

Wishing to apply a severe teaching to those who followed Him closely, He said with irony:

"It is not good to take the bread of the children and cast it to the dogs."

Dogs was a term used for those who were not part of the chosen Israelites.

The expression "*dogs*" sounded like a tender admonition. The strong image spoke for itself.

The Canaanite woman understood that her condition would not present her with another opportunity. She suffered and resigned herself to that.

However, her maternal love speaking louder, she replied assuredly:

"Yes, Lord, but the young dogs also eat from the crumbs that fall from the table of their masters!"

Undoubtedly, His message was destined for Israel, where the harshness of the Law and pride reigned supreme; however, His kingdom would include the whole Earth…

Through that dialogue He wanted to impart the power of humility as a teaching that would be inscribed in the spirit of the disciples.

Exulting with the firm trust of the Canaanite and her lofty simplicity, the Master does not ask for her belief or her origin, does not reproach her life or reprimands her pleas. He speaks to her only with love:

"O woman, great is your faith. Let it be done for you just as you wish."

* * *

The first reaction of the Just One had been odd in ignoring the affliction of someone who implored His help. His attitude of apparent indifference, however, was intended to touch the heart of the disciples. Yet, they did not intervene on behalf of the suffering woman, evidencing an unfortunate habit they seemed to still cultivate.

The tenderness, the sincerity and helplessness of that mother had touched the Lord.

Exuding mercy, from a distance the Rabbi expelled the obsessing[29] spirit that controlled the young woman in a prolonged process of mediumistic phenomena, and afterwards, undeterred, He continued on His way.

The example that it is possible to cure from a distance, analogous to the case of the son of the Centurion, is sustenance for all peoples, for the men and women of the future.

The vigorous words and the austere life of Jesus were bound to reach the multitudes of all times that did not have, like Israel, the bliss of His physical presence. The Israelites, however, who did not receive Him, in turn would experience long periods of harsh trials as a consequence of their folly – a fire whip on their conscience to exonerate them.

* * *

Arriving home, the Canaanite woman very happily found her beloved daughter totally recovered.

The seed of hope the Rabbi had placed in her heart transformed into a radiant lamp that illuminated her for the rest of her life.

---

[29] "Obsession, which is the domination that certain spirits acquire over certain individuals." Allan Kardec, *The Mediums' Book*, Ch. XXIII, #237. – Tr.

THE SAMARITAN WOMAN

Samaria no longer enjoyed the glories of its past, the times of Ahab's and Jezebel's magnificence and impiety. Destroyed in 722 BCE by Sargon II, brother and successor of Shalmaneser V, the Assyrians moved the exiled peoples from all parts of the Empire to Samaria's mountainous region, creating an amalgamate of races and beliefs.[30]

In Esdras' time, after the 935 BCE split[31] following the death of Salomon, a Zion priest not connected to the Temple erected an opulent sanctuary on Mt. Gerizim to rival with the Temple of Jerusalem.

Destroyed by the Maccabees led by John Hyrcanus in 128 BCE Samaria had been rebuilt by Herod, who called it Sebaste or Augusta.

---

[30] Jn. 4:1-42. – Spirit Auth.
[31] Israel in the North and Judah in the South. – Tr.

In a canyon almost 600 meters[32] deep, between Mt. Ebal and Mt. Gerizim, an old village was located named Shechem,[33] better known as Sychar.

The historical small town had known Patriarchs and Judges, and had seen Joshua gather the "chosen people" there to pledge fidelity to the Covenant...

Having departed Jerusalem the day before toward Galilee, Jesus left the royal road between Jericho and Batanea along the tranquil waters of the Jordan River. He climbed the mountains of Ephraim instead, thus entering the borders of Samaria, a place avoided at the time by those born in Judah.

The rough, pebbled trail suddenly would be colored by swaying oleanders and branchless sycamores through which, as the biblical language conveys, at sunset the trade winds refreshed Yahweh himself in his garden.

Golden wheat ears oscillated in the warm wind of the sixth hour[34] in the immense field sprawled over the valley.

The dust, accumulated along the steep winding road, would lift light clouds in the air blowing down from the spikes of the scorching mountains.

From the summits, in between slim hills, the sea could be seen in the distance.

The sinuous soil coils and writhes between the mountains until it flattens out in the verdant valley.

White raggedy clouds glided over the vastness of the blue sky.

---

[32] App. 1,968 feet. – Tr.

[33] "Back." – Spirit Auth.
The Hebrew name Shechem is probably derived from the word for "back" or "shoulder" – an apt description of Shechem's location in the narrow valley between Mt. Gerizim and Mt. Ebal. www.jewishvirtuallibrary.org. – Tr.

[34] Noon time. – Spirit Auth.

The journey had been long for Jesus and His disciples – approximately 50 kilometers.[35]

A dry throat and a tired body covered in dust ask for refreshing crystal-clear water.

Arriving at the skirts of the city, the Rabbi sits down next to the traditional "Jacob's well" in the lands that belonged to this venerated patriarch – later bestowed to his son Joseph— and where he had been buried.

While the disciples had gone to the city to get food and fruit, Jesus sunk into deep thinking in the midst of the colorful landscape.

* * *

A water jar on her shoulder, immersed in her own problems, a woman comes to draw water in the scorching midday sun.

She is startled by the peculiar gaze of the foreign Jew, who seemed to be waiting for her.

Nonetheless, she lowers the jar down to the water and collects the precious liquid.

She is anxious, as if something was about to happen to her.

Unknown emotions agitate her spirit.

As she picks up the water jar to return home, she hears: "Give me to drink!"

Astonished, she turns, overcome by strange and profound feelings.

Why does that *foreigner* dare talk to her in defiance of existing customs? She asks herself mentally. What man is this who dares talk to a woman knowing that no one else would

---

[35] App. 31 miles. – Tr.

have the audacity to do so in public, not even to a wife, a daughter, or a sister? Did he ignore this simple rule, this basic aspect of all social duties? Letting out her own anguish, she responds shrewdly, some irony in her voice:

"How is it that you, being a Jew, are requesting a drink from me, a Samaritan woman?"

In the valley, the month of May sang through a thousand cicadas in the wheat field, the deserted and quiet road meandering up into the mountain.

Jesus knows well the dissensions that separate both these peoples: the Jews and the Samaritans.

This would not be the only time He would provoke a *scandal* by affronting the odious conventional customs.

He has a message to give – a message of conciliation and consolation.

For this reason He had purposely left the road along the Jordan River and had climbed the mountains. He had programmed that encounter since a long time ago…

That woman, He had chosen her to be the carrier of His message to Shechem.

He answers her without harshness or censure, perhaps because He knew her inside.

His voice is melodious and compassionate.

"If you knew the gift of God, and who it is who is saying to you, 'Give me to drink,' perhaps you would have made a request of him, and he would have given you living water."

Unparalleled vibrations pulsate in the woman's heart.

She yearns for peace but did not know how or where to find it.

A doubt, however, concerns her.

Her astonishment gives her voice a tone of respect.

"Lord, you do not have anything with which to draw water, and the well is deep. From where, then, do you get this living water? Surely, you are not greater than our father Jacob, who gave us the well and who drank from it, with his sons and his cattle?"

The eyes of the stranger glow with an unknown magnetism.

The revelation is about to be announced: the message will be dispersed in the air, rocking the world once He proclaims it.

"All who drink from this water will thirst again. But whoever shall drink from the water that I will give to him will not thirst for eternity. Instead, the water that I will give to him will become in him a fountain of water, springing up into eternal life."

"Lord, give me this water," she said hurriedly, "so that I may not thirst and may not come here to draw water."

Did she really understand the deep meaning of the words of the Rabbi? Did she want only to free herself from the exhausting task, or was she seeking more understanding of the teaching?

His gentle eyes glimmer and settle on hers, penetrating the inner depths of her spirit.

"Go, call your husband and return back here," He commands her with firm tenderness.

She becomes perturbed.

She was a sinner and He knew it, she concludes…

This was her inner torment.

How wounded and humiliated she felt, how fearful!…

Abundant tears stream down her face; words weakened the vigor of her lips, and almost out of breath, she explains:

"I have no husband…"

Shame displays her pain on her tanned face.

"You have spoken well, in saying, 'I have no husband'," confirmed Jesus, "for you have had five husbands, and but he whom you have now is not your husband. You have spoken this in truth."

Surprised, the Samaritan woman does not contain her happiness and joy.

She almost screams:

"Lord, I see that you are a Prophet!"

Her mind is in turmoil.

All her life she had had so many doubts! ... And now she stands before a Prophet from God. She must take advantage of each minute, she must renew herself, she must find peace at last.

Uplifted, she inquires with docility.

"Our fathers worshiped on this mountain, but you say that Jerusalem is the place where people ought to worship."

"Woman, believe me," elucidates the Divine Envoy, "the hour is coming when you shall worship the Father, neither on this mountain, nor in Jerusalem. You worship what you do not know; we worship what we do know. For salvation is from the Jews. But the hour is coming, and it is now, when true worshippers shall worship the Father in spirit and in truth. For the Father also seeks such persons who may worship him."

The perplexed woman is filled with joy.

She considers herself so unworthy, but nonetheless she had been called to hear the Truth, listening to what no other ear had heard before.

In the valley the wheat ears continue to sway, oleanders singing in the blowing wind.

The Stranger looks at His surroundings, and continues in His melodious voice:

"God is Spirit. And so, those who worship him must worship in spirit and in truth."

Did the humble "water gatherer" comprehend the universal greatness of the teaching?

Transfigured by the revelation, she wants to be reassured and asks:

"I know that the Messiah is coming (who is called the Christ). And then, when he will have arrived, he will announce everything to us…"

The imposing symphony bursts forth from the heart of the Master, and with Nature silent and expectant, He concludes:

"I am he, the one who is speaking with you! For this reason I say that salvation will come from the Jews."

Sweat runs down his bronzed virile face.

The secret has been revealed.

The floodgates of mystery have been shattered and truth spreads happiness and consolation.

Silence was broken.

The woman has been persuaded.

The Kingdom extends its frontiers among the "astray"…

* * *

The disciples return and "marvel that He had been talking to a woman," but said nothing.

Taking her water jar, the Samaritan woman goes back into town and proclaims loudly:

"Come and see a man who told me all things that I have done. Is he not the Christ?"

Questions erupt spontaneously from those surprised at the unaffected announcement of the woman.

In compact groups, Sychar residents flock to the water well where the Rabbi is sitting among the disciples that are urging Him to eat.

Unperturbed by the crowd that looks at Him with astonishment, He explains to His disciples loud enough to be heard by everybody:

"I have food to eat which you do not know. My food is to do the will of the One who sent me, so that I may perfect his work…"

"Do you not say, 'There are still four months, and then the harvest arrives?' Behold, I say to you: Lift up your eyes and look at the countryside; for it is already ripe for the harvest. For he who reaps, receives wages and gathers fruit unto eternal life, so that both he who sows and he who reaps may rejoice together."

"For in this the word is true: that it is one who sows, and it is another who reaps.'"

"I have sent you to reap that for which you did not labor. Others have labored, and you have entered into their labors."

The approaching sunset dressed the earth in red and the clouds in hues of gold.

The message is an awakening call for the hesitant and negligent learners.

He sows, the future will harvest.

The human arable field is right there, with plenty of hearts for the sowing of the New Era.

It was necessary to extend to all the prelude of peace, in a preview of the Kingdom.

The listeners were shepherds, farmers, fishermen…

They understood the language; they knew the times and circumstances.

Hosannas to God would no longer be sung only in this or that enclosure...

Erecting an altar in the heart, the farmer will praise Him in the field covered with germinating seeds, the artist in the art piece rich in contours, the wise in the poems to the stars, the lowlier in the performance of humbler endeavors...

The light comes from Above and extends throughout the plains...

All hatred disappears with the New Message.

Barriers are shattered, abysses are flattened.

Chains of enslavement are broken and apathy does not strive.

Peace burst forth in all hearts.

Wherever humankind rises to life, the Father is worshiped.

God no longer belongs to one people, to one caste. Immanent in everything and everyone – God is transcendental.

"One God and Father of all, who is over all, and through all, and in us all."[36]

The *here and now* is no longer important in light of everlasting joy.

The loathing of crime, frivolity and the folly that widely and easily incites a titanic inner battle for equilibrium, the perseverance in the formidable effort of preservation of the good, the renunciation to the sickly and ambitious focus on the "I" – these are the prelude to happiness ... for those who dedicate themselves to the Cause.

The recompense is the peace with oneself and the ineffable bliss thereafter, beyond the shadows...

* * *

---

[36] Ephesians 4:6. – Spirit Auth.

He stayed in Samaria for two more days: preaching, curing, spreading the certainty of Life after life.

In the meantime everybody would say to Photina[37]:

"It is no longer because of what you said that we believe; for we have heard for ourselves, and we know that this is indeed the Savior of the world."

The diaphanous heaven was sprinkled with splashes of small clouds when He and His disciples at last departed for Galilee.

* * *

For the affection she devoted to Jesus, early Christians, encouraged by her bravery in proclaiming her imperfections, called her the *Samaritan Woman* – "The Enlightened One," which oral tradition espoused and upheld to our days.

---

[37]   St. Photina, one of the martyrs of early Christianity. – Tr.

CHAPTER 10

AMBASSADORS OF HOPE

Bethabara or "House of the Ford, Place of Crossing" was located in a ford of the Jordan River, a place where caravans stopped overnight after crossing the river on their way to distant cities.[38]

The news arriving at the village would gather strength there and, carried by eager travelers, would reach faraway places.

John the Baptist had been there calling for repentance, symbolically washing away the sins and "opening the pathway for the Lord."

In the festive air that invariably characterized these encounters now hovered the tragic news of the decapitation of the "Baptist" in Machaerus, in the arid region of Perea.

A profound sadness, filled with bitterness and resentment, could be seen on most faces, as perhaps they recalled the benefits they had received from the Precursor Apostle...

---

[38] Lk. 10:1-24. – Spirit Auth.

With the end of the Festival of Booths,[39] groups of travelers stopped in the cities along the way to visit relatives, to talk, to reminisce...

That particular month of Tishri[40] had been quite exciting.

During the Festival in Jerusalem, the Jewish hatred had increased, tightening its grip around the figure of the Messiah.

The cold nights and days fostered the gatherings in Bethabara, as it did before during the preachings of John the Baptist.

Two years prior the Rabbi also had been on those sites, and His soul was still infused with the sublime emotions He had felt at approaching the fresh waters, letting Himself be baptized so that "what was written would be fulfilled."

His stay this time would be longer. Perea needed Him...

He passed the days listening to the afflicted, tending to the sick, offering the guidelines to the Kingdom.

The rains were strong at that time of the year, spread by powerful gusts of wind.

$$* * *$$

They arrived in groups, originating from many different locations. They turned up throughout the day, descending the banks of the river in the direction of Bethabara.

They showed in their faces the unspeakable joy of a task accomplished and a duty fulfilled.

---

[39] Also known as the Festival of Sukkot, it begins on Tishri 15, the fifth day after Yom Kippur. The word "Sukkot" means "booths," and refers to the temporary dwellings that [Jews] are commanded to live in during this holiday in memory of the period of wandering. www.jewfaq.org. – Tr.

[40] October. – Spirit Auth.

Their hearts sung psalmodies, anxiously waiting for the time to give their account of the happy moments of the journey they had undertook.

These men had not solely visited the populous cities and traveled the royal roads. They had been in villages and had climbed mountain trails opened by goats. They had taken turns in the apostolic zeal, clearing the ground and preparing the sowing.

They had gathered listeners on the shores of the lake, the market squares, and next to the tents…

Now they were eager to relay their experiences.

The foggy morning disguised the region's normally scorching sun, the trees surrounded by the heavy mist. The rains had stopped and the wet soil seemed to exult in hope, as if anticipating a blissful sowing.

They anxiously awaited the Rabbi, who had left to tend to the needy nearby.

And while they waited, they reminisced…

The Master had made friends among those who listened to Him. Everybody was a beneficiary of His love, and they would do everything to prove their gratitude to Him. They exulted in joy at hearing Him preach.

After choosing the Twelve who would be in charge of spreading the Promise of the Kingdom to come, He had proceeded to call them from among those in the multitude who listened and loved Him, telling them poignantly:

"Certainly the harvest is great, but the workers are few. Therefore, ask the Lord of the harvest to send workers into his harvest."

"Go forth. Behold, I send you out like lambs among wolves!"

"Do not choose to carry a purse, nor provisions, nor shoes."

"Into whatever house you will have entered, first say, 'Peace to this house.' And if a son of peace is there, your peace will rest upon him. But if not, it will return to you. And remain in the same house, eating and drinking the things that are with them. For the worker is worthy of his pay."

"Do not choose to pass from house to house."

"And into whatever city you have entered and they have received you, eat what they set before you."

He gazed upwards and became silent for a few moments, as if consulting the Father. After a brief pause, He continued:

"And cure the sick who are in that place, and proclaim to them, 'The kingdom of God has drawn near to you'."

"But into whatever city you have entered and they have not received you, going out into its main streets, say: 'Even the dust which clings to us from your city, we wipe away against you. Yet know this: the kingdom of God has drawn near'..."

As His mouth enunciated these sublime recommendations, the golden rays of the sun shone high in the clear sky.

The arid lands of Judea contrasted with the green fields of Galilee and the rich crops bordering the lake.

They had departed with their spirits bursting with indescribable emotions... And filled with joy, they were now returning...

* * *

Philip, who had been called to spread the seeds of light, had asked to first "bury his father"; and now he was back there, attentively listening, moved to tears, hearing the eloquent account of the joyous harvesters. Afterwards he would evangelize Samaria and Saron as a deacon, accompanied by his four daughters, all prophetic-mediums of the Early Church.

Matthias, who would replace Judas after the tragedy of the Cross, at seeing the Master arrive approached Him with the others and stated exultingly:

"Master, our hearts are filled with joy, like dates drenched in honey."

"Happy are you who were able to till the soil of spirits!"

"Those who listened to us seemed to be listening to You; the words in our mouth became enriched with eloquence and harmony, delivering an inspired wisdom that perturbed the shrewd and cunning. It was as if we were taken by the Holy Spirit!"

"Fortunate are you for offering conditions to the Truth..."

Recalling the events, in a calm voice filled with lofty emotions, the disciple continued, enraptured:

"No one rejected us anywhere. The demons obeyed amenably, and many of the formerly possessed would kneel in front of us, worshiping us as the pagans do before their idols. Astonished, we would enlighten them!"

"Be cautious and watchful. Evil is obsequious and conceit poisons the spirit. 'I know well what you did. I saw the Unclean Spirit plunge, attracted to the abyss,' but that is not enough..."

"We experienced no thirst, no hunger, no pain. In Your name we raised the paralytic and opened blind eyes closed to the light by laying our hands over them, invoking You..."

"Behold, I have given you authority to tread upon serpents and scorpions, and upon all the powers of the enemy, but still that is not enough..."

"Not a few stood up singing hosannas after we explained the days we live in, what we heard from You, what we have seen..."

And after a brief pause, the disciple concluded:

"… Our souls sing with happiness and our hearts rejoice!"

Extending his gaze toward the emotive crowd and wishing to keep the guidelines of the nascent Gospel steadfast and dignified in all hearts, the Master turned to the triumphant returning disciples and concluded:

"Yet truly, do not choose to rejoice in this, that the spirits are subject to you; but rejoice that your names are written in heaven."

And as everybody drew nearer to hear Him, the Rabbi prayed serenely:

"I confess to you, Father,
Lord of heaven and earth,
because you have hidden these things from the wise
and the prudent,
and have revealed them to little ones.
It is so, Father, because this way was pleasing before you."

His eyes glowed like a celestial dawn, the cold wind stirring his tousled hair. His slim face became transparent and illuminated as if an unknown light had been lit within, exuding diaphanous translucence.

Heartily, He continued in a strong and crystal-clear voice:

"All things have been delivered to me by my Father.
And no one knows who the Son is
except the Father,
and who the Father is,
except the Son,
and those to whom
the Son has chosen to reveal him."

Unknown melodies sang in the cold wind.

Lowering His voice to the musicality of tenderness, He spoke especially to the Twelve Apostles and to the Seventy disciples gathered for the spreading of the Good Tidings:

"Blessed
are the eyes that see
what you see.
For I say to you, that
many Prophets and kings wanted to see
the things that you see,
and they did not see them;
and to hear the things that you hear,
and they did not hear them."

A heavy silence fell upon the assembly.

The trees swayed lightly.

The sound of the Jordan River, widened by the floods, could be heard in the proximity.

The Master left.

The Seventy and the Twelve retired to their tents.

The listeners scattered.

* * *

From among the Seventy called to spread the Words of Life were Barnabas, who would later collaborate effectively with the Apostle Paul; Sosthenes, who would also cooperate in the letters to the Corinthians; Cleophas, who encountered Jesus on the road to Emmaus...

Their "names recorded in heaven" in order to unceasingly serve the Cause of the Truth while periodically returning to the Earth.

A thousand times they would be invited to exemplify the gentle manner of lambs among wolves in the evolutionary pathway.

They would continually reincarnate in the flesh throughout the centuries, recalling the teachings of the Rabbi, bearers of fervent speech and glittering writing, invested with the resources to submit the Spirits of Darkness, preparing the days of the Consoler in the future ahead. But most of all, to exemplify the Gospel, put aside with the passing of times, so as to maintain it vigorous and alive until the moment of the reconstruction of the World, the moment when the magnificent symphony will be sung by the voices of Heaven...

CHAPTER 11

THE TABOR AND THE PLAINS

The force of their reality could depict them as a diptych: the blessings of God on the mount, the conflicts of humankind in all their vigor on the plains.[41]

From the heights of the Tabor, where they communed with the excellences of God, Jesus, Peter, James, and John descended towards the spiritual flat land of humankind.

Resplendent, minutes before the Master had been surrounded by a powerful light and dialogued with the venerable ancestors of the Jewish people: Moses and Elijah.

Emotions had not yet subsided to their normal level, and already the downward curve of suffering was taking devastating shape in the everyday reality of human contingencies.

On the summit, the vision of real life; at the base, anguish and suffering.

"Deaf and mute spirit, I command you, leave him; and do not enter into him anymore," Jesus exhorted in a firm voice in which compassion blended with energy.

---

[41] Mt. 17; Mk. 9; Lk. 9 – Spirit Auth.

There had been no argument. Everything had been simple, the brief scene culminating with the young man lying on the ground unconscious, disfigured and drenched in cold sweat, as if he were dead.

Moved, the Master had bent down. Touching the forehead of the no longer possessed young man, He lifted him up with a captivating gesture.

He was almost a boy…

From a very young age he had suffered under the violent and cruel yoke of the discarnate persecutor. The roots of such horrible hatred were lost in the shadows of the past, a time when they had acted as accomplices in the broad banquet of insanity, entangled in an odious bloody episode… Now the sovereign law that tied the unpunished criminal to the affronted justice was in full manifestation.

The discarnate "spiritual parasite" had attached to the sufferer, reproducing in the possessed the epileptic seizures that were consuming him, the persecutor, ultimately also a victim of himself, enslaved in his own hatred. Consumed by his vengeance, exerting total control over his victim, the spirit would throw the young man to the ground, set fire to his clothes, and try to drown him.

In their attempts to find a cure, impossible up to that moment, the hopes of the family had faded away like a lamp without oil.

His father, helpless while the young man continued on the way to inexorable annihilation, had heard of the Rabbi and had brought him there, in spite of the doubtful expectation of his son's cure.

* * *

Eight days[42] had passed since "Peter's confession." The Master "took Peter and James and John, and He ascended onto a mountain."

August in full force pours its cup of light and heat over the earth. Scorched poppies and daisies fall to the ground, their stems bent by the heat wave. The sky, very blue and transparent, allows for infinite views in all directions.

As the Tabor[43] is ascended, the landscape unfurls: at the base the fields of harvested wheat, the brownish blur of the Jordan River resembling an immense lute between shrubberies; to the East the towering Gilead Mountains, and to the West the sparkling waters of the Mediterranean, similar to an enormous mirror, reflected through the natural gorge between Mt. Carmel and the high peaks of Lebanon; to the North the Lake of Gennesaret sprinkled with colorful sails, fringed by Tiberias, Magdala, Capernaum, and Bethsaida, the towns dressed in green palm trees enchantingly cascading over the small hills in the direction of the shores...

From the summit the vision is unhindered. Circular, its platform beaten by the winds and sometimes crowed by junipers, it is the culmination of 562 meters[44] of rocky terrain without much vegetation, standing out in the large and beautiful Galilee.

Night was still some hours away before extending its vast mantle under the sky. The months of August are made of long days. The heat is suffocating and scorches the sparse vegetation.

---

[42] Eight normal days are taken as "six full days, according to Jewish customs." – Spirit Auth.

[43] Historians and exegetes argue the location of the transfigurations, whether it happened on Mt. Tabor or Mt. Hermon. We prefer the tradition that situates it on the former. – Spirit Auth.

[44] App. 1,843 feet. – Tr.

The journey is long towards the top of the mount: more than four hours of slow and tiring climbing despite the beauty of the dazzling surrounding landscape.

Once at the summit, the Master starts to pray. The disciples, sweaty and tired, fall asleep in the shade of the scarce shrubbery.

A great silence involves everything and everyone. The heat is almost asphyxiating...

Nightfall engulfs nature and the Master prays.

Dawn finds the Rabbi still praying. His companions sleep. Voices are heard in the silence. Startled, the disciples wake up and are mesmerized by the sublime vision of the transfiguration of the Master, his clothes white as the light, dialoguing with Moses and Elijah. Words vibrate in the air; but these are not words normally heard...

Once the vision dissipates, Simon Peter approaches the Rabbi and says:

"Lord, it is good for us to be here. And so, let us make three tents: one for you, and one for Moses, and one for Elijah."

The Masters looks at him with compassion.

A mysterious cloud appears and a voice then proclaims: "This is my beloved Son. Listen to him!"

The disciples, still bewildered, become terrified.

The great revelation had taken place.

Jesus appearing in all His glory and they had been the silent and moved witnesses of the incomparable event.

The Heavens had split open and the disciples had been imparted the "knowledge of the Divine."

Much later Peter will report this *metamorphosis* of the Master, the undeniable testimony upon which he supports his faith.

The Rabbi, however, requires them to be silent about it.

Truth needs to be conveyed in small portions so as to be understood by the human clay.

John would later write down the "sayings of the Lord," starting his narrative by evoking the unforgettable scene: "Life was in Him, and Life was the light of men. And the light shines in the darkness, and the darkness did not comprehend it."

* * *

"Let us go down," says the Master.

"Could we stay a little longer?" asks Peter.

"It is necessary to go down," replies Jesus. "We must seek those who don't have the strength to climb up. Humankind needs us. Theirs is our glory. May our bliss be theirs, and their suffering be ours. After communion with Heaven the convergence with those who are on the Earth. Paradise would be a strange prison without those who, in the shackles of their afflictions, yearn for the land of freedom. Let's go down! Humankind, for whom I have come, waits for us."

* * *

They talk throughout their descent.

"Rabbi!" They ask fearfully. "Why then do the scribes say that it is necessary for Elijah to arrive first..."

"Elijah has already arrived, but they did whatever they wanted to him. So also shall the Son of man suffer from them..."

The disciples then understood that He was speaking of John the Baptist.

The new revelation that Elijah had reincarnated as John the Baptist surprises the disciples, who start to begin to understand the inscrutable designs of the Father.

The spirits are exulting in happiness. Their hearts are filled with bliss.

* * *

Jesus and the disciples continue their descent.

The day is resplendent. These last events shine like suns in their souls.

The summit of Mount Tabor is left behind.

Large expanses of land extend below.

They hold the suffering and anxious humanity, as well as the rest of their companions.

On the plains, scared, the disciples are taking turns.

"Leave him, Satan!" shouts an angry Judas while the possessed howls.

"Son of darkness, seed of Beelzebub," screams Thaddeus in a hoarse voice and bloodshot eyes "leave your victim!"

"Evil, unclean spirit," bellows a pale and sweaty Nathaniel, "I command you to return to the depths of hell! ..."

Some curious bystanders approach the screamers while the young man possessed, as if multiplying the strength of the spiritual vampirism that consumes him, becomes even more irate, thrashing and kicking on the ground, imperiling the weakened convulsing body almost completely defeated.

"This is Dibbuk[45] itself!" wails Philip, discouraged.

"We won't be able to do anything!" concludes de son of Clopas.

---

[45] In Jewish folklore and popular belief an evil spirit which enters into a living person, cleaves to his soul, causes mental illness, talks through his mouth, and represents a separate and alien personality is called a *dibbuk*. www. jewishvirtuallibrary.org. – Tr.

"Where is the Master," asks Simon the Zealot distressingly, "that He does not come to help us? Can He not see our difficulty?..."

Trembling, they look at each other while the possessed foams from the mouth and tosses on the ground.

They all talk at the same time. They scream in vain.

Seeing the Master and His companions approaching the mire of human miseries, they run to Him in distress and greet Him.

"What are you discussing with them?" asks the Lord serenely.

"Teacher, I beg you, look kindly on my son, for he is my only son. And behold, a spirit takes hold of him, and he suddenly cries out, and it throws him down and convulses him, so that he foams. And though it tears him apart, it leaves him only with a struggle. I asked your disciples to cast him out, and they were unable!"

"If you can," pleads the father, "save my son!"

"If you believe it, everything is possible to those who believe."

"I believe, Lord! Help my incredulity."

The Rabbi is moved. His serene countenance expresses all the sorrow in His spirit.

Without any bitterness, He looks at His fearful companions and admonishes them with vehemence and compassion. He understands the weaknesses of those invited to spread the seeds of the Good Tidings.

As if to justify himself and the others, Judas tries to explain:

"We did everything You taught us but could not achieve anything..."

"How long will I be with you and endure you?"

The question hovers in the air without a response.

The arrogance of weakness is more petulant than the vanity of might.

The sign of failure in one's pride burns like a blazing sore.

"Deaf and mute spirit..."

Pallid and extenuated, the young man smiles, a deep gratitude without words. He kisses the hand of the Rabbi, and led by his father, ecstatic with joy, they both returned to their home.

*   *   *

At night, as the firmament dressed itself with sparkling stars, still under the impact of the Master's demonstrations on the Tabor and the plains, Simon, possibly conveying the visible disquiet of the others, approached Jesus while He meditated and asked clearly disturbed:

"Why could they not expel the unclean spirit?"

"This kind is able to be expelled by nothing other than prayer and fasting," clarified the Master.

However, wishing to use the moment to better instruct the inattentive and pretentious companions, the Lord explained further:

"Before anything else, it is necessary that we understand that the *unclean spirits* have lived before, that they were men and women and continue to be so. As misguidedly as they lived in the flesh, they continue their insanity outside of the body. Death has not transformed them. Travelers in time, they are what they made of themselves. Mentally connected to the reminiscence of their deeds, they continue to suffer and experience them, tied to those they loved, attached to those who made them suffer..."

He briefly paused and then continued:

"For this reason the Good Tidings are a hymn of love and forgiveness: unconditional love and impartial forgiveness."

"For brothers and sisters in the darkness of ignorance there is no other power than the power of love. Not only expelling them from the connections that link them parasitically, but also to succor them, involving them with love…"

He silenced once more, involving His companions with kindness, and then continued:

"They are our brothers and sisters still ignorant of their reality, lost in the illusions of the flesh to which they stubbornly imagine to be attached. They did not prepare themselves for the truth. That is the reason why the Message of Life is not clothed in the fancies of general liking. It is a seed of light to sprout in the soil of the spirit."

"Therefore, in dealing with the possessed and the possessors only prayers of indefatigable love and the fasting from passions are able to mitigate the thirst that devours them both, delivering them to the workers in the Labors of Our Father who, everywhere and unceasingly, are cooperating with the endeavors of Love."

* * *

"If you love instead of hate, if you wish to succor the spirits instead of only expel them, you will be able to, since everything I do you can also do, and even more if you so wish…"

Soft breezes danced in the light air of the night, scattering into the future the words of the Rabbi in a glorious preview of the forthcoming days for Humanity.

CHAPTER 12

THE DEMON-POSSESSED GERASENE

The sea was an immense gently rippling mirror, darting golden rays that reflected the particles of light of the nascent Sun.[46]

The month of Kislev,[47] a carrier of storms, is also the messenger of abundance, the carrier of light and fragrant breezes.

Soft noises can be heard in the surroundings as the desolate escarpments of Gergesa or Gerasa are left behind.

The dark and slippery cliffs, beaten by sea winds, are dreary and devoid of any vegetation. It could be said that it was an ungrateful soil, where nothing thrives with the exception of thorns and wild thistles.

On the top, groups of men, women, and children extending their gaze over the liquid face of the sea, a precious concession of the Jordan River along its blessed course, inquire without words.

---

[46] Mt. 8:28-34; Mk. 5:1-11; Lk. 8:26-39. – Spirit Auth.
[47] December-January. – Spirit Auth.

The boat glides softly, almost in silence, its great billowing sail similar to a flying wing casting its shadow over the waters.

At the stern, the figure of Jesus can be seen, a deep expression of sorrow on his face. Gazing at the rugged and bare land, He feels the suffering of the people that live there.

Since times before, He had programmed that visit to the lands of the mountains of Bashan in the Decapolis, wishing for the possibility of introducing the message of the Good Tidings.

To proclaim and spread the prelude to the Kingdom was His bliss, the purpose of His coming: to live among the people, to suffer the afflictions of the people, but above all to enlighten and free their spirit from the vigorous shackles of ignorance and superstition.

The people were His flock. He came to give His life to this flock. But it was necessary for the sheep to know their shepherd in order to identify His voice and answer to His calling. Instead, He was now suffering deeply because the people did not understand Him – a suffering deriving from love that has been rejected.

Gerasa did not receive Him, despite the festive announcement of His arrival and the precious offering given by Him as He approached its borders.

Did He not break the shackles that attached the obsessed to the obsession, like a clear shining ray that penetrates the darkness of the night and announces the power of its presence?

The Gerasenes traded with swine and preferred the pigs to Him, the Friend they wished to ignore...

A melodic wind crests the waters, lyrical tunes vibrate in the sorrow that engulfs the boat and tousles the thick hair of the disheartened silent men.

Gerasa had inflicted a great sadness upon them…

* * *

Someone asked on the small cliff plateau, looking at the boat disappearing in the distance:

"Who was that?"

"We don't know" replied someone else.

"Why did he want to talk to us? Was he bringing us something?"

"We did not ask, we did not even let him speak."

"What did he want from us?"

"We have no idea. Maybe it was for the best to have expelled him from our lands as we did."

"Perhaps!..."

And as they gazed once more at the boat, a small dot in the middle of an interrupted message, a woman suggested:

"He looked like a Rabbi, like those who wander through Galilee…"

"What good can come to us from Galilee?" snapped a furious city authority. "What we are certain of are the losses he forced on us."

"And where is the possessed?" inquired another.

"Let's look for him!" responded an incensed young man. "Let's make him confess. After all, he's the one with the unclean spirits and with him we can be severe."

"Let's be careful", advised a swine merchant. "The damages of this day are enormous; we lost our best swine herds and this will affect the wealth of our city. The sick young man seems to have recovered. Let's leave him alone…"

The boat was now an almost invisible speck in the sea.

The day embroidered the earth with light, nature displaying an exuberant feast. A thousand onomatopoeic voices sang a song of happiness.

From the cliffs of Gergesa one could see the other side of the sea.

The Gerasenes returned to the city, two kilometers[48] from there, its houses of Greek architecture surrounded by rich pastures extending to the borders of the desert.

Jesus and the disciples returned to Capernaum.

* * *

He remembered how simple it had been.

Dawn had not yet removed the thick dark nightly mantles to reveal its light when he heard the sound of footsteps within the terror that was his life.

He had stood up in the empty tomb, from the many that existed in the caves formed in the rocks among the hills used as crypts.

Suddenly he had felt the force of the *furies* that controlled him in a heinous and wicked subjugation.

He had an idea of what he had done by the welts and bruises in his aching body and limp limbs, the taste of blood in his mouth and the exhaustion that overpowered him…

He thought of how low he had fallen! The games of pleasure in dens of perdition had brought him to that state. Tormented by subjugating forces, he had abandoned his home and relatives after lifting the cup of unnamed bitterness to the lips of his parents, who succumbed in shame and horror in the maze of their sufferings.

---

48 App. 1.24 miles. – Tr.

He had started to slip very early on, ending up rolling with the pigs and seeking the darkness of the tombs where the demoniacs sought shelter, filthy pieces of rope and an iron link hanging from his wrists and ankles, like those used to tie wild animals...

Remembering now the turpitudes and sufferings, he could not stop the copiously flowing tears.

He had roamed the nearby woods, fighting with animals over food, or, completely deranged, he had spent endless days in indescribable battles, fighting with the *wild beasts* that were pounding him...

Gathering his thoughts, he could only remember the refreshing breeze that involved him, and those serene and kind eyes that had immersed him in amenable harmony.

"Lord!" he had whispered, nervous and feeble, soaking in sweat. "What do you want me to do?"

"Return to your house and explain to them what great things God has done for you."

"I don't have anyone," he had replied. "My close ones hate me for all I made them suffer. Let me follow you, since you had pity on me."

"No, not yet! First tell them what you have been given so all will know what the Son of Man can do."

He had jumped to his feet and had run from there, followed closely by the owners of the swine that had plunged down the cliff. However, he had no idea how these *things* had happened.

He was free. Free! He shouted, exploding in happiness. And he smiled.

The others looked at him with fear, hearing without believing, despite the sanity he seemed to be showing now.

Legion, that's what he was called, the many unclean spirits that possessed him making him feared and detested.

His explanations, however, and the eloquent evidence of his recovered lucidity were all in vain. When Jesus approached the city gates, they received Him without consideration or respect and expelled Him right away.

In the following days, wherever he went, the young man spoke of the promise of the Son of Man.

The Gerasenes, however, angry that they did not benefit from His presence and His aid, harbored a silent resentment against the formerly possessed young man, which finally exploded in widespread hatred:

"Since he cured you," they would say arrogantly, "and is more valuable to you than to us, go to his side and leave us and our lands."

The hatred of the masses, like a rogue hurricane, pulls everything in its way into its vortex.

"Go away," the voices screamed. "Leave us alone!"

A stone cuts through the air, blotches of warm blood stain the soil, dust turns into mud on the ground.

The eyes of the recently cured young man turn red, his mouth twisted in a strange contortion, as he cries out:

"Damn you, Gerasa, who expels your sons and disdains the celestial Envoys!"

The voice thundered powerfully, and the city that witnessed the scene of shame and pain would not forget what had happened and the expression of the two men to whom it had closed its doors.

* * *

After wandering through the lands of the Decapolis, telling how the Galilean had cured him, he went to the shores of the other side of the sea and joined the multitudes that followed the preachings on the lake and the towns, the hills and the side of the roads, offering his hands and his arms to the afflicted and the sick in need of help.

He would never turn away from those who suffered, his brother and sisters in misfortune.

He sought to give them the treasure of hope as he himself had received it from the Rabbi.

He followed Him, with wonder and gratitude, giving what he had received and loving how he had been loved, working for the expansion of the Kingdom of God announced by Him.

CHAPTER 13

BE CLEAN

Joy exploded in his heart, as if a waterfall had just surged, playing a thunderous symphony.[49]

It occurred so suddenly.

He saw Him in the distance, coming down the mountain, followed by a multitude.

He seemed to be haloed by a strange light.

An aura of serene tranquility surrounding Him.

Then something had happened inside him.

Unknown courage impelled him forward.

Up to that moment he had been a deranged animal, hunted and on the run.

Prohibited from entering the cities, he roamed the fields, almost always in the company of other miserable wretches like him.

When the first purple spots appeared on his tanned skin and the nauseating and painful pustules started to decay his body, he also started to die...

Everybody chased him away.

---

49 Mt. 8:1-4; Mk. 1:40-45; Lk. 5: 12-16. – Spirit Auth.

Ties to the family had been broken and the dreams of his youth had turned into heinous darkness.

Hounded, he had been excluded.

Name, origin, everything stayed behind.

Now he was only one thing: *unclean*!

The bitter suffering killed his faith and destroyed his hopes.

A displaced person in his own cradle of birth.

An outlaw without a crime.

Living among animals, he covered himself with the mantle of the starry nights and filthy rags; and amid the fury of the winds and the pouring of the rains he fought for caves with the beasts and for leftovers with the dogs…

He had lost the ability to cry.

He had become numb.

He felt only his own pain, profound and cruel, flogging him relentlessly.

* * *

"Lord, if you are willing, you are able to cleanse me! I believe you are the One we are waiting for. Say: I will!…"

Tears flooded his eyes for the first time in many years. His voice died in his swollen throat.

"I am willing: be cleansed!"

A nervous tremor jolted the fibers of his being, his broken body shaking uncontrollably.

He wanted to scream, was unable to.

An overall penetrating transformation was taking place.

Dumfounded, unable to reason, he just followed in utter astonishment the swift renewal of his organism's febrile and rotting tissues.

His body was once more a diamond under the miserable tattered rags.

He flung himself to the ground, "his face down," and screamed haltingly:

"What do you want ... me ... to do?"

Oh, infinite joy!

His entire being trembled with jubilation.

"See to it that you tell no one. But go, show yourself to the priest, and offer the gift that Moses instructed, as a testimony for them."

The strange Rabbi had become diaphanous. An unparalleled beauty radiated from Him. He seemed to smile.

The crowd came closer and, speechless with amazement, verified his cure.

Ecstatic, emotions in disarray, he left running.

Mind in turmoil, heart beating wildly, he returned to the city...

Before, he was expelled with stones. Now, singing with joy, he was returning.

Along the way, however, unable to keep his silence, he kept announcing the miracle that had happened to him.

* * *

Night had fallen without much notice.

Under the light of the distant stars the Master gathered the disciples in a friendly circle.

At meal time, with the warming fire ablaze, bread and smoked fish were shared by all. Approaching the Rabbi, Simon asked with curiosity:

"Was it necessary for the leper to pay the tribute[50] to the Temple?"

"For the fulfillment of the Law," replied Jesus.

"Legally, he had been dead. Brought back to life, by the mercy of Our Father, he must be recognized by those who represent tradition. We do not see the tribute as a pure and simple payment or homage, but as an expression of evidence of re-entry in the society of men."

Piqued by curiosity, Andrew asked:

"Is the recommendation for silence justified? Is it not necessary for all to identify the signs of the Message of Life so that people prepare for the Kingdom of God that is near?"

The Master lifted His gaze as if to get a hold of His surroundings and replied:

"Not long ago I spoke to you about the salt of the earth... What good is the salt if it loses its flavor? By diluting it in the food it makes itself present without fanfare and everybody can taste it..."

And after a brief pause, as if to better illustrate the days to come, He clarified:

"The Kingdom of God will not be noticed through external attractions. The Earth has always had plenty of prodigious men and women, prophets and rabbis, healers and soothsayers. Above them all, however, the Son of Man has always watched."

To further enlighten the incipient disciples, He continued:

"The leper cured today had contaminated himself spiritually in a near past. Yesterday, arrogant and selfish, he

---

[50] [Jews] were required to pay the annual half-shekel tribute to the temple. www.bibleodyssey.org. – Tr.

had drenched himself in the tears of the oppressed, abusing his body like the wild winds on lone tamarinds. He returned to the pathways of torment, he himself tormented, to painstakingly repay. The gift he received today, much more than merit, represents responsibility. The merciful Father does not desire punishment for the ungrateful or rebellious child, but its renewal…"

As if listening to the light whispering of the night, He concluded with a sorrowful tone in His voice:

"Not all, however, are able to understand."

"This very moment, patting his rehabilitated flesh, he shows his body to the curious and speaks about the One he does not know with joy and levity. The most important healing he did not experience: the healing that is not restricted to form but to the spirit. Cleansed of the morphea, he continues to be a leper. Be watchful of the contagion of the miseries that the eyes don't see, but which darken reason and perturb the heart…"

Simon, wishing for more explanations, asks respectfully:

"Rabbi, if the sick could not benefit from the cure, would it have been useful?"

"Simon," replied Jesus kindly "the Kingdom of God is a message of love for everyone: the disheartened and sufferers, the tormented and the sick, they all will receive the invitation in accordance with their necessities. It is up to us to spread the gifts of light and blessings without any immediate concern of how they will be received or used. Each heart is responsible for the seeds it gathers. Enjoying the gift of light, each one can choose where to enshrine hope. The Sun spreads life everywhere indistinctively and, while the swamp continues to be putrid, the king star still insists on shining on it, despite its pestilence and death, always sowing hope…"

He stood up and, with the group in silence, and He went into the night and disappeared.

The mountain in the back continued to be shrouded in darkness.

As the beads of the minutes continued to form the chain of the centuries, the events of that day would be passed on to the everlasting days of tomorrow...

CHAPTER 14

THE HEMORRHAGING WOMAN

The arrhythmic heart constrained her chest, and the thick air she inhaled seemed to be filled with smoke.[51]

An incoercible anguish pressed upon her spirit since the day before.

The night had been difficult. Unparalleled expectation had beset her since she had heard the dreadful events at the Garden of Olives…

The betrayal of Judas had been followed by the desertion of His friends and Peter's denial while He, completely alone, had been the object of scorn and arrogance, led to the extreme humiliation by those who, for a long time, had been wanting to get their hands on Him.

The news, intoned like a wearisome cantilena, was scornfully repeated by all lips, even by the mouths that had been lifeless before and could now speak thanks to Him.

The day had started with a scorching Sun that burned everything.

The hot wind at that hour was searing.

---

[51] Mt. 9:20-22; Mk. 5: 25-34; Lk. 8: 43-48. – Spirit Auth.

The sinister procession that shoved Him in the direction of the Golgotha had not yet left the gates of the city, the mob further increased by the impenitent spectators that had welcomed Him just days before at His arrival in Jerusalem.

She hears them scream: "Get on! Flog him!"

She feels her own heart ripping apart.

The hill is hard to climb and the mockery continues, the lashing whip tearing His bloodied flesh...

Covered in blood and sweat, helped by Simon of Cyrene, He proceeds slowly, with great difficulty.

She loved Him! Yes, she loved Him with all the strength of her heart, of her life. She was living because she had received life from Him.

Eyes filled with tears, she looked around. In the crowd she could see Mary, His mother; Magdalene, weeping desperately, her hands clenched; Joanna of Chuza, Mary of Clopas, Salome, Martha and John, all of them seized by indescribable suffering. Perhaps, farther away, stunned and defeated, there might be others: Nicodemus, Zacchaeus, Joseph of Arimathea, Lazarus, as well as the blind and the paralytic who had recovered their health...

Screams and imprecations intensify...

* * *

Disillusioned, for the very first time she had left her city of birth, Caesarea of Philip, in the Decapolis, marked by the humiliating stigma.

Everybody considered her impure and consequently unwelcome.

She had tried all healing approaches. She had consulted the priests, local and foreign physicians, all to no avail. The cruel infirmity resisted all types of medicines.

She had been exorcised, had followed the precepts of the Law, had submitted to procedures that had harmed her endlessly, everything in vain. Her *malady* was a punishment, a sign of misfortune imposed by God.

Without any more hopes, after spending everything she had, she had decided to go to prosperous Capernaum in a futile attempt to get a remedy not yet used or to consult a physician not yet seen.

The *blood flow*, however, did not leave her.

She felt constrained to hide, to conceal the sign of her misery.

Now, for the first time, she had the opportunity to speak to Him.

His name, His prodigies, she knew them all by those who, through His hands, had recovered their health as a supreme gift.

And now He was there, just a few steps away.

He was walking towards the house of Jairus, the Synagogue leader, whose daughter was in the throngs of death, with the whole city lamenting that irreparable loss.

Loved for his kindness and understanding of human problems, Jairus had looked for the Rabbi everywhere since the early morning. He had gone to Peter's house, then the house of the sons of Zebedee, and lastly he sought Him at the beach after traveling to the other side of the sea. Along with Jairus, a large and curious crowd was also following Him.

She was among that crowd and now, just two steps away from Him, she felt crushed by an unmatched anxiety. She lacked the courage to speak to Him, there were too many eavesdropping ears close by. They knew her, the marks of her physical misery denouncing the *malady* that had made her so extremely timid. Anemic, emaciated, even in front of doctors she felt the embarrassment inflicted by the *infirmity*.

At that decisive moment, however, if she lost her chance she would lose the most precious, the most important minute of her life.

Her mind in turmoil, she got closer, emotional and fearful.

She believed in Him. He touched her deeply, as if an unknown miraculous force radiated from Him. His eyes, His bearing, His whole being emanated such great serenity and grandeur!...

The narrow street, the crowd intensifying and closing in, her inner turmoil screaming without a sound, pleading for help without words.

Overcoming her agony, with blurred vision, in an irresistible gesture she pulled the edge of his cloak, and ... Oh! What bliss! The blood flow stopped, the hemorrhoids no longer hurting, a strange and unusual feeling passing through her.

Before she could regain her bearings, she heard Him ask: "Who touched my cloak?"

His disciples replied: "The people are crowding and pressing in on You, and You ask who touched you?"

He looked around as if seeking for her.

She then threw herself at His feet, confessing:

"It was me, Lord, I was so miserable! I knew that in touching Your garment I could regain my health."

"Daughter," He addresses her with tenderness and kindness, "Daughter, your faith has saved you. Go in peace and be healed from your *malady*."

The ineffable emotions of that moment! If she could, she would have stayed there, motionless, in gratitude and tears of joy, worshiping Him.

She soon was awakened to reality by those who had witnessed the event.

A few days later, she returned to her loved ones and the places she had left on the other side of the sea.

Everybody wanted to see her, hear her, verify.

With her recovered health came an unstoppable hunger for a new life. She had regained the peace of body but had lost the peace of spirit.

After knowing Him, she had encountered life. To be away from Him meant to lose it once more. She knew it, *something* was telling her that He was the celestial Envoy! She needed to leave everything and follow Him...

After some reluctance, she said goodbye to her friends and relatives – who so much had despised her before – and went to Him.

Since then, lost in the crowds, she had followed His preachings on the shores of the sea and the nearby towns.

Slowly her spirit was filling with peace, like the light of the Sun floods the earth on the wings of the dawn.

Following Him everywhere, she was aware of those who despised Him, and in her heart she was fearful for Him...

* * *

The imprecations woke her up from her reminiscences.

The dolorous reality came back with the loud clamors of hate and widespread tumult.

That cruel climb on the slope of the Accra debilitated Him under the weight of the cross.

Suddenly He slipped and fell. She could no longer hold herself back: she took the white towel she was carrying and ran towards Him.[52]

They were not quick enough to stop her.

Those features, bloodied and wounded, broke her heart. She covered His face in the white linen and wiped it tenderly.

General stupefaction when she removed the towel: His face was imprinted on it tinted with blood.

She cried:

"Look at this, all of you! Help me!"

Weeping, her voice falters...

"The whip!" shout the Jews, "the whip! Flog Him without pity!"

He, however, looks deeply at her in that split second. His opened lips say nothing, but she hears inside of her His voice, as she did before:

"Go in peace! I will remember you..."

The procession crosses the Law Court Gate[53] on the slope and starts the ascent toward the Hill of the Skull.

He falls down once more.

The loud anguished plea of the women can be heard.

---

[52] While the *Acts of Pilate**(one of the apocryphal gospels) inform that this woman, Bernice or Veronica, is the same hemorrhaging woman, Eusebius of Caesarea, the historian, declares that following her cure the woman with the blood flow had returned to her place of origin and had the event with the Master cast in bronze to be displayed in front of her door – something that he himself had seen. However, we prefer the information contained in the "Acts of Pilate." – Spirit Auth. [* Also known as *The Gospel of Nicodemus.* – Tr.]

[53] The gates of Israelite walled cities typically had three chambers with four sets of "doors." It is likely that these chambers served as "offices" for city administration, including the "law court" (either formally in criminal cases or less formally as the place where family business or disputes were settled). www.bible.gen.nz – Tr.

Macerated and trembling, He magnetizes the crowd with a wounded gaze and says:

"Daughters of Jerusalem, do not weep over me. Instead, weep over yourselves and over your children. For behold, the days will arrive in which they will say, 'Blessed are the barren, and the wombs that have not borne, and the breasts that have not nursed.' Then they will begin to say to the mountains, 'Fall over us,' and to the hills, 'Cover us.' For if they do these things with green wood, what will be done with the dry?"[54]

Once the top of the hill was reached, they started to disrobe Him...

Soon after He was dead.

At the foot of the cross, remembering His deeds, she then recalled His words:

"And when I have been lifted up from the earth, I will draw all things to myself."[55]

He was lifted.

Humanity would follow Him later.

She came down from the mountain and continued to serve Him along with those who loved Him.

---

[54] Lk. 23:27-31. – Spirit Auth.
[55] Jn. 12:32. – Spirit Auth.

CHAPTER 15

ZACCHAEUS, RICH IN HUMILITY

Set apart, the Publicans[56] or tax collectors constituted a despised class, living under an outpouring of hate and sarcasm.[57]

Their livelihood, acquired with the sweat of afflictions, was filled with the anguish of those constrained to payment of heavy taxes imposed by the victorious hosts dominating Israel.

Jericho was a famous city, a center of commercial activities. In the past it had hosted Cleopatra, who had been enchanted by its light and fragrant air.

---

[56] The Publicans in Israel obtained from the Roman conquerors, through a public auction, the right to collect taxes for five years, many times going too far by charging exorbitant customs and land taxes. They were divided in three distinct branches: *Decumani* (collected thites); *Partitores* (in charge of customs houses); and *Pecuarii* (received taxes for land and pastures). They were managed by the acquirer of the rights of levies to whom they rendered obedience and with whom they united as they were disparaged by their compatriots. Seen as ignoble for their allegiance to the foreigners and for infringing the Law and Moses, on the other hand they were also detested by the invaders who underrated and humiliated them with reproaches. – Spirit Auth.

[57] Lk. 19:1-10. – Spirit Auth.

Beautified by Herod and Archelaus, its sumptuous buildings and palatial marble mansions stood out for their austerity and beauty of lines.

Located in part in the Jordan valley, on torrid days it benefitted from wind gusts and refreshing breezes, while on cold days the temperature remained amenable without any significant lows.

Known for its commercial center, it was chosen by merchants, money exchangers, pilgrims, and caravans traveling to the many countries of the East, dispersing at sunset the aroma of its abundant roses scattered everywhere.

Fields and prairies shaded by sycamores, its pomegranate and almond trees were sprinkled with strong red and golden-yellow flowers. Plateaus covered with wheat and sugarcane rivaled in splendor with the terrain, colored by abundant wild flowers that gave it an air of smiling and springtime beauty. The tamarinds, the most celebrated of Israel, were of three different species, its dates the sweetest flavor of honey.

Its customs houses were always packed, *business* reaching high and expressive figures.

Jericho, splendid, with its thriving economy, was located on the way to Jerusalem...

* * *

Zacchaeus, through public auction, had acquired the right to collect taxes in Jericho, and along with them, their cursed legacy.

Residing in a sumptuous palace, he had amassed a fortune, adorning his domestic abode with art objects from many countries, surrounding himself with opulence in order to fill with external goods the emptiness of his heart, knowing that he was detested by the entire city.

Of an affable disposition, however, he justified his *trade* by saying that not few of the sons of Israel had competed with him before the emissaries of Caesar.

As much as he could, he tried to dissipate the heavy clouds of ill will and hostility that darkened his days.

Attempts upon attempts, however, proved futile.

Even when he doubled his efforts the response was always discouraging.

He would listen somewhat aggravated to the threats uttered through clenched teeth by those who were obliged to fulfill the disgraceful duty of paying tribute to Caesar through him...

Of small height, which only added more distress to his anguish, and overweight, Zacchaeus was the living example of the city's idiosyncrasy.

Often, while caressing his children, the tormented Publican considered the future and made plans... Once he'd have enough wealth and been able to quit the ignoble activity, he would leave the city, start a new life away from Jericho, far, far away ... A smile would rise to his lips and a hardly contained hope would fill his heart, giving him the strength to withstand all the tormenting suffering he was going through. The future belonged to him. He only had to wait a bit more...

Zacchaeus had heard of Jesus.

The news reaching his ears seemed more like a message of love and hope. It seemed unreal to him that someone could love that much. He, Zacchaeus, was also thirsty for love. He yearned for affection, for friends... He longed for ostensible expressions of friendship, the large smiles of understanding and acceptance...

The information that He ate with sinners and even talked to Publicans brought inner tears to Zacchaeus. And the tears flowed stronger when his workers at the customs house told him that, without a doubt, among those who followed Him fervently there was one, a Publican also, that He had pulled from a tax collecting house...

Admiration and affection inspired Zacchaeus toward that Stranger!

Sometimes during his reflections he yearned to see Him, to hear Him, to talk to Him. Deep down inside he believed that He was the Messiah.

His words traveled through the air, His deeds belonged to everyone, were known everywhere.

The unfortunate, those forsaken by hope, the downtrodden, the *proletarii* loved Him! And those who hated Him feared Him, because in Him they recognized the Savior!

* * *

Bartimaeus, the blind beggar, had lived in Jericho for as far back as Zacchaeus could remember.

Holding his miserable platter, he begged in the streets and the country roads.

At the customs house Zacchaeus frequently helped him. He liked to help the poor, to alleviate pain, as he knew all too well the sorrow of loneliness. They, the sufferers, did not refuse his friendly alms, the same alms the puritans and defenders of the Law refused to offer them, showing in their countenance of false purity their constant expression of loathing...

Bartimaeus, blind and despised, had something in common with him, Zacchaeus: the loneliness they both felt, even in the middle of the crowds.

* * *

On a certain March afternoon in 30 CE, Jericho had become festive. For some days now the city had been hosting pilgrims for Easter, which would be celebrated in all its pomp in Jerusalem.

That afternoon, however, the bustle was unusual.

Word had spread that the Rabbi had cured Bartimaeus's blindness, and that the formerly despondent man had entered the city gates singing hosannas, showing his clear eyes bathed in an indefinable light.

Miracle! Some exclaimed.

Fraud! Shouted others enraged.

Everybody wanted to talk to the former blind man, they wanted details.

In the middle of the natural commotion resulting from the hectic chatter, someone hollered in a frantic voice that the Galilean Rabbi was approaching and soon would arrive in the city!

An emotional turmoil shook Zacchaeus soul. He could barely contain himself.

The Awaited One was coming!

This was his moment, the most precious moment in his life.

He needed to see Him.

He certainly would not dare speak to Him, but…

If he lost that chance … never again! Oh, he would never again have another one!

Breathless, abundant cold sweat running down his face, putting aside the dignity he normally imposed on himself, he started running in the direction of the city gate.

The crowd on the road was getting larger.

It was imperative to see Him, to just see Him, to see Him walk by.

Distressed, taken over by a thousand anxieties – knowing full well that he would not be able to see Him because of his height, that others would be in front of him on the road, and that, despised as he was, no one would trade places with him – at a glance he saw an accessible old and bare sycamore tree on the side of the road, its rough and curved roots protruding from the ground.

The Publican did not hesitate. Resolute, he ran towards the tree and climbed it.

He saw the Master, serenely approaching, surrounded by the crowd.

Shouts erupted in praise for the strange Walker, who seemed involved in a diaphanous light...

Zacchaeus let the voice choking in his throat come forth crystal-clear and, without noticing it, he joined in the general excitement.

How striking was the Rabbi! He had never seen beauty like that, filled with majesty and translucence!

The Lord stopped his step next to the sycamore and looked at Zacchaeus.

It was very quick, but in that instant the whole life of the tax collector rushed explosively through his mind.

He assessed himself...

"Zacchaeus," said the Sublime Visitor, "hurry down. For today, I should lodge in your house."

It could not be true. He was dreaming! His ears were ringing, his mind went hazy. "Hurry down" his spirit shouted to him inwardly.

He slid down the tree, transfigured by emotion, alone, removed from everything else, as if he were floating in the fragrant air of the afternoon. He wanted to smile, to show acquiescence. He could not, unable to speak or to act.

His brain seemed like a live blazing coal.

He knew he was rich – and the rich were despised.

A Publican – the Mosaic Law condemned him.

He felt unworthy – and Israel would never forgive him...

But the Voice continued to command: "today I should lodge in your house."

He broke away from the torpor and rushed back home. It was crucial that he prepare the reception.

Tears poured from his tired eyes, his heart beating vigorously after such lengthy loneliness. His wife, embracing him, also wept.

He sought a way to become humbler in the opulence of the grand house and to become worthier in the humility his afflictions had placed him, in order to receive the Rabbi, his Only Friend...

It was almost night time.

A golden fringe embroiders the mountains in the west with light, pouring an iridescent fan of feathers that adorn the nimble passing clouds...

At the door of his villa, with his family at his side, Zacchaeus waits with great emotion.

He is fearful, however, that the Rabbi will not enter his house.

He does not feel worthy of hosting Him, but would do anything for such honor.

"Lord!" shouts someone. "Are you going to spend the night at the house of this Publican?"...

Publican! (The word echoes in Zacchaeus' ears.) The label etches a blazing pain in his aching and anxious heart!

"Behold, Lord," stammers the tax collector, "one half of my goods I give to the poor. And if I have cheated anyone in any matter, I will repay him fourfold!"

He could not continue. Pale and temporarily unable to speak, an overwhelming emotion prevailed over him.

Jesus smiled, a smile light and kind like a scent of love.

"Today," He said softly, "salvation has come to this house; because of this, he too is a son of Abraham. For the Son of man has come to seek and to save what had been lost."

After a brief pause, in which the sounds of the arriving night could be heard, the Lord narrated the unmistakable parable of the ten minas, using as the preliminary imagery the Israelite prince Archelaus, who "traveled to a far away region, to receive for himself a kingdom, and to return …"

Zacchaeus made himself humbler and became worthier.

He submitted to humiliation and glorified himself in humbleness.

* * *

Narrators of evangelical events declare that, many years after the epic of the Cross and at the request of Simon Peter, the former Publican had gone to lead a nascent Christian church in the lands of Caesarea, rich with love and humility, guided by Jesus…

CHAPTER 16

THE FAMILY OF BETHANY

Surrounded by vast fields of barley, small groves of olive and fig trees that give shade to the Jericho meandering road close to the city walls, Bethany was an hour from Jerusalem.[58]

From the Golden Gate, the road of Jericho reached Cedron, contouring the Mount of Olives before continuing towards Bethphage.

The scenery in Bethany differed greatly from the opulent bustle of the city of the prophets.

Despite "the thunderstorms of Cheshvan,[59] so similar to the sound of trumpets," which pour down so suddenly, the light and translucent air allowed – as it still does today – to see far into the distance. To the south in the direction of the lands of Moab, or to the northeast above the hills of Gerasa, the serene sky and the transparent air always offered an incomparable view.

The humble village seemed to contrast in its greenness with the harshness of Judea, to which it belonged.

---

58   Lk. 10:38-42. – Spirit Auth.
59   The month of November. – Spirit Auth.

The scenery was bucolic: carpets of small flowers over the green grass, the crown of the Mount of Olives in the distance tinting the dazzling landscape with the gray-green color of its trees.

The slopes covered by vegetation displayed little white houses with flowering porches.

Although close to the capital, in reality it was far away from the pageantry and bustle of the great city.

* * *

The quiet town of Bethany was an amenable refuge after the tiring journeys.

Many times Jesus had sought these sites to reinvigorate His heart and to uplift the hearts of others.

That October of 29 CE, as the first thunderstorms rolled in and the tempers in Jerusalem flared, the Master set out towards enchanting Bethany.

The web of intrigues kept tightening its threads.

Sanhedrinites lurked everywhere, scattering spies on the Rabbi's path.

They wanted to catch Him in blasphemy.

Jesus, however, unperturbed, continued the sowing of the truth.

He knew that human beings were "spiritual children," and that hate is the result of frightened untamed love.

If on one hand spite and envy weaved the odious threads of implacable persecution, on the other the fine strands of love enveloped many valorous and dedicated Spirits.

In Bethany, Lazarus and his sisters Martha and Mary were the proof of this eloquent love.

Unafraid of the Pharisees or the murmurings of their timid and fearful neighbors, they gave shelter to Jesus in their home, surrounded by fragrant roses and built of walls covered by climbing vines. Surrounding it, cedars and blooming peach trees created a charming post card in which the little house stood out with its large porch and columns hugged by dark green ivy.

They loved Jesus and would say so openly. They had made Him a member of their family, and to receive Him at their house was the same for them as engraving a star in their domestic bliss.

Many of these loving friends would soon be entering Jerusalem singing hosannas, would follow the procession of the Cross, would do the climb towards the Golgotha, would be dazzled by the Resurrection, and then would travel to Galilee for the last instructions before His ascension... After which they would continue heroically, following the footprints left by the Master, expanding the hopes for the kingdom to come...

To these friends He loved so much Jesus offered the most expressive treasures of light and life.

Lazarus himself, who dedicated to Him the purest of friendships, will be pulled from the dark shadows of catalepsy some months later by Him, when called from afar by the weeping sisters, at the sepulcher covered in funeral clothes, reeking of miasmas...

Crowned by diaphanous golden and violet tones, the mounts and hills have quieted down in the arms of the sunset. Soft fragrances rise from the cool valley.

The *voices of nature* sing a pastoral song.

The transparent air moves softly.

In the houses the first lamps start to glimmer with a red-yellow glow.

With the end of the Feast of Tabernacles (Sukkot) in Jerusalem, after the challenges had been faced with valor, Jesus and His disciples needed rest.

The Master was aware of the difficulties, and the Twelve found themselves fearful sometimes.

In concert with the golden sunset, the silvery moon adorned the firmament.

Alerted by a disciple that had walked ahead of the others, Lazarus jovially waited for the Rabbi and His closest circle at the door of the graceful and open little house.

"Peace be in this house," said the Master.

"Peace be with You, Master," replied Lazarus with an effusive embrace while he kissed the face of his beloved Guest.

The two sisters rushed to receive the visitors, serving them water for the ablutions, the house filling with the ensuing natural chatter.

Martha hastily turned to domestic chores, preparing the meals, making the beds, setting the table... Breathless, taking care of everything, she looks for Mary, calling her.

While outside the sounds fade and the night silently sets in, the Rabbi tells Lazarus the latest news and what lies in the future.

Mary, seated at His feet, looking at Him tenderly enraptured, follows His every word.

"Mary!" calls out her sister.

And at finding her, Martha complains:

"Master! Tell her to help me. While I tire myself (she smiles affably) she bothers You, not helping me prepare the house for the meal."

"Martha, Martha," replies Jesus smiling, "Martha, Martha, you are anxious and troubled over many things. And yet only one thing is necessary. Mary has chosen the best portion, and it shall not be taken away from her."

Disappointed, Martha quieted down while the Lord tenderly narrated:

"A married man received the news that a King would come to his home. He prepared the house with his wife. When the Monarch arrived, he drew near to hear and honor him, while the wife rushed to complete other small arrangements. But the King could not stay long and after a light repast, he left. Only those who listened to him got acquainted with the plans for his kingdom, which was the more important part..."

"Forgive me," Martha justified herself, "these are old, deeply rooted habits."

"To reach plenitude," added the celestial Friend, "only one thing is needed: a strong spirit capable of breaking the old shackles and, once renewed, to surrender completely to the *things* pertaining to the Celestial Father."

"You are right," agreed the hostess.

"Bread and clothing, the earth gives us that," clarified Jesus. "The starry sky is an optimal blanket and the gentle soil is a sacred granary. The word, however, is a seed of life. Concern with immediate things characterize the earthly plane in which many get lost, perturbed by the turmoil of their own struggles. The incessant search for the truth, exchanging multiple *things* to acquire just one inner peace with spiritual security – that is the liberating vertical aim."

"As if they were in a cruel labyrinth, men and women tire themselves pointlessly and lose themselves, because they ignore the capital differences between real and imaginary values."

"Some shackle themselves to possessions and are controlled by what they have. Others encase themselves in their passions and succumb under their weight. Numerous others cling to ambitions and lose sanity following their dangerous paths."

The Master glanced around.

The lighted room was framed by the darkness of the night.

Attentive and curious, the hosts and the disciples listened in silence.

After a brief pause and with more emphasis, the Master continued:

"The victorious of the world, while in the flesh, are restless, and after crossing the threshold of the tomb feel defeated and afflicted, tied to the moorings they left behind. Only those who can triumph over the world and its illusions ascend vertically towards spiritual glory without hardship. For this reason 'the Son of Man has nowhere to lay His head, despite the birds of the air having their nests and the wolves and serpents having their holes.' Disdaining all things, He centers on just one: to love everyone indiscriminately so that the kingdom of understanding, in perfect communion of ideas, is promptly established among the creatures of the earth."

"Lord," asked John, very moved, "will it take long for this hour of human understanding to arrive?"

"The seeds," replied the Master, "are being scattered now. The blooming and harvesting belong to Our Father. Let's sow, all of us, loving one another, tirelessly and without haste, and enraptured by the truth let's advance, resolutely, for this is all that is needed."

Outside soft fragrances were spread in the gentle wind that lightly stirred the trees, while the stars, like curious onlookers, spied from afar...

CHAPTER 17

THE RESTORED-TO-LIFE WOMAN FROM MAGDALA

Seated at the entrance of the sepulcher carved in the rocks, her emotion bursting out in tears, she asked herself: what had happened? Where could they have taken Him and why did they remove Him from this site in the quiet of the night?[60]

Gradually her concern grew into desperation.

The Sun shone through the grayish clouds, the cold wind stirring the few anemones and sporadic roses amid the shrubbery.

In her mind echoed the voices of the lads in white who told her: "Do not be afraid. For I know that you are seeking Jesus, who was crucified. He is not here. For he has risen, just as he said ..."

She believed that the Master, as He had said, would rise from the dead. She was afraid, however, that the Jews could have taken his body.

---

[60] Mt. 28:1-10; Mk. 10:1-11; Lk. 7:36-50 and 24:1-11; Jn. 20:11-18; Acts 1:6-8. – Spirit Auth.

Scared, Joanna of Chuza as well as Mary, the mother of Mark, and the other women went down to the city to convey the disappearance of the body of the Rabbi.

Peter and John anxiously climbed the hill and saw for themselves: the strips of linen with the embalming aromatic substances in the empty tomb, the kerchief, the stone moved aside...

Terrified, the two disciples returned to the city with the sad news; she, however, had stayed behind weeping.

The events of the last few days had been dolorous and surprising. She could neither understand nor make sense of them.

A longing coupled with pungent grief pierced her heart.

And then everything happened very fast. She had the impression of a lightly fragrant, gentle breeze passing by.

She turned her head and amid her tears, a few meters from her, she saw a man who asked her:

"Woman, why are you weeping? Who are you seeking...?"

That voice! That profile! She could not finish her thought.

"Mary!"

"Rabboni!"

She was completely stunned. The Master was alive and right there, radiant like the nascent sunrise!

"Do not touch me. For I have not yet ascended to my Father. But go to my brothers and tell them: 'I am ascending to my Father and to your Father, to my God and to your God'."

The golden morning light shone on his glowing garments, and a myriad of small suns seemed to be incrusted in Him.

She was overjoyed. She wanted to express with words her unparalleled sentiments, like the sorrow she felt until now. She could not speak, however; her voice had died in her tight and constricted throat. "Go to my brothers and tell them..." These words reverberated in the depths of her spirit.

She stood up. Smiling and without any hesitation, her soul singing hymns of joy, she took the road to the city that was just waking up.

The light air of the morning embalmed with the last scents of the night, the green fields of Acra and Bezetha beyond, the landscape framed by the Sun and the pinnacles of the mountains trimmed in gold – that was the sublime scenery in which He had returned.

She overcame the distance feverishly and reached the cenacle where the brethren were gathered, withdrawn and fearful.

The sad shadows of sorrow hovered in the sad ambient.

As soon as she walked in, she announced in a joyous voice:

"I saw Him! I saw the Rabbi! The Master has come back to those who love Him!"

She smiled and cried at the same time. Stammering, her face reddened by the emotion, she continued:

"He told me to announce Him to His brothers. He will rise towards the Father. Listen to me: Jesus lives!"

All the fibers in her body were trembling, as if they would come undone.

Her voice vibrated harmonies that found no receptivity in the hearts of her companions, those she had gotten to know from the daily familiarity of the last few weeks.

"Tell me, daughter," asked Mary, His mother, anxiously, "tell me everything. Did my son return?"

The voice trembled from understandable emotion.

"I don't believe it," shouted someone among them. "The Master has died and left us in this difficult situation, all alone... I don't believe in His return. Only if I see Him myself..."

She looked around the room with teary eyes to find who had doubted.

He walked toward her, his face taut in an expression of anger and disenchantment. Before she could say anything, he stood between her and the other perplexed and stunned companions, snapping:

"Even if He returned…"

He paused briefly.

" … who would He present Himself to? Certainly to Simon who He had elected to lead us; or to John, to whom He always showed His love; or to His mother…"

The sarcastic and scornful tone of his cutting words displayed all the bitterness of his tormented and unhappy spirit.

And after a wider pause, to the astonishment of all the others, he continued:

"… But instead He chose to appear to you? No, I don't believe it. Let's not believe her. It is not possible that He would have appeared to her. Weren't others at the tomb? Weren't Peter and John there? Why her? …"

It was as if a torrent of ice and discomfort had fallen over everybody.

An uncomfortable silence fell upon the room.

She stepped back.

The doubts struck her like cruel stabs. "Her?" "Why her?" like acid burning her over and over again.

Even so, with great effort, overcoming her own suffering, she replied with a feeble voice:

"It is true! Even if you don't believe it, I saw Him. In spite of my former disgraced condition," she muttered humiliated, "the Rabbi has appeared to me a little time ago…"

"I believe it, daughter," emphasized His longing Mother. "An inner feeling tells me that my Son is alive. I believe it because our grief and hearts are with Him, just as His heart is with us."

She embraced her tenderly, seeking to hear her out with caring kindness.

Mentally Mary Magdalene retraced her own pathways – how long and how tortuous they had been!

Many a times she would feel these blows. It was natural that they doubted her. She felt completely rotten. Had it not been for the call of the Rabbi and her life possibly would have ended in complete degradation or total destruction. And in the days to come she would time and again shed the bitter tears of recovery for her past days of folly.

It is common to proclaim virtue, she thought, while hindering its spread.

How many new temptations she was trying to sublimate only she knew.

It is easy to reproach error, but few are those who extend their hands to uplift and support the victims of ignorance and criminality.

Not that she wanted to justify herself.

Her conduct had been reproachable. Indeed shameful, she recognized it.

In Magdala her name and her villa were an integral part of the degrading scene of the city.

A while ago she had settled there...

* * *

Magdala was a very prosperous center of commerce and industry, all sorts of merchants and adventurers from the East flocking to the city. Set on the edges of the sea, it enjoyed an amenable climate and privileged fish-abundant waters.

A resting resort, it received illustrious and aristocratic Greeks, Romans, Babylonians, Phoenicians, and Medes who sought its comforts, lucrative deals and easy pleasures.

Adventure-seekers naturally converged there, along with courtesans with tired bodies who displayed in sumptuous villas the merchandise of their own suffering in nights of orgy and madness, on the road of total moral decline.

After painful and rough experiences, she had been able to acquire a lavish palace in the famous city, surrounded by gardens and a vast orchard where old and austere sycamores shared the grounds with oak trees, rosebushes, and small honeysuckle.

Her house hosted the most requested men transiting though the busy metropolis.

She was very young; the liquor of youth ran freely, intoxicating and seductive, attracting rich buyers who competed for the vanity of its possession.

Night time had always been her discreet accomplice. Once darkness fell and lamps and torchbearers were lit, the old oak door on the external walls would give access to those who, in the public streets, through prejudice and hypocrisy, would dispute the *honor* of stoning her if such an occasion arose…

In her residence of sober Greek lines she possessed everything that ambition could covet: exotic expensive jewelry, rare perfumes and unique extracts in vessels of engraved alabaster, Persian and Babylonian rugs, cedar chests filled with silks and damasks, furniture of artistically carved mahogany, coins of all origins, servants from many different lands… Everything vanity proclaims to produce happiness. But she felt neither happy nor blessed.

In the immense residence, filled with precious things, she felt empty, tormented and vulgar.

Her wealthy condition did not change her status as a miserable harlot, a merchant in the commerce of illusion.

She suffered unspeakable anguish.

In long and sorrowful nights of loneliness, she seemed to hear scornful voices scoffing at her misfortune, almost always experiencing the incomparable torments of an obstinate spirit-obsession in her tired and aching body and mind.

It was said that she was possessed and she feared it to be true.

The women beyond her walls, perhaps happier than herself, envied and at the same time loathed her, while men perturbed her with their pursuit.

She yearned for inner peace in the midst of the immense abyss of destructive passions and she desired love – a strange love – a love she secretly craved for without ever finding it.

The love she knew was nothing more than lust and unhappiness.

She believed in love made of peace and tenderness, total surrender and serenity. She did not expect, however, to find it. She was utterly unhappy, anticipating not too far in the future the savagery of some cruel or tyrant warrior, or the stones of false respectability in the public square…

A generous heart, she liked to help, and because she was unhappy she understood the sorrow of other sufferers, taking pity on the afflictions of the downtrodden. From her adorned hands and fingers poured coins and bread, and while her doors were frequently closed to the seekers of pleasure, her servants had strict orders to open them to the pain and suffering in search for help or shelter.

When her mind was calm, in festive dreams and raptures she would go back to a happy childhood, only to be startled afterwards by her caustic reality.

* * *

His name reverberated in the acoustic of hearts like the soft melody of a harp played in the distance.

The pain flees at the contact of His hands and light infuses dead eyes; a spiritual joy permeates those who are around Him and a strange and sweet hope stirs the hearts wherever He is – this is what all the voices proclaimed.

Her servants talked about Him with a strange rapture in their eyes, formerly dull and listless. They called Him the *Liberator*, and added that he was not a common liberator, like those who promise to break the iron shackles of political and social slavery, but a peculiar savior who offered perennial peace and a total liberation: serenity and inner security independent of physical circumstances.

In the squares, the beaches or on the roads the multitudes followed Him enraptured, as if He exhaled joy in those harsh days of trials and misery.

On a night of springtime fragrances, urged by a trusted and devoted faithful servant, she allowed her to speak about Him.

Her heart was heavy and she felt the cold constriction of the unknown forces that hounded her spirit, perturbing her reasoning and embittering her days.

The young servant, who had heard Him speak the day before, said confidently:

"Mistress, He will spend the night nearby, in Capernaum. Go and see Him!"

Her voice was almost pleading.

In her mind twirled the fantasies of her desperation, but even so she considered:

"But your Rabbi, will He receive me?" She asked, loathing herself. "Rabbis are pure and abhor the wretched, raising their voices to threaten with penance and punishment those who, like me, have plunged into the abysses of disgrace…"

"The Rabbi," eagerly explained the young woman, "loves the sufferers and speaks with everyone, saying that impurities many times are hidden and no one sees them, but that everyone is worthy of understanding and help."

"But I am different. You know *what* I am… (Hot and comforting tears, which she had not experienced in a long time, began to flow.)

"Mistress, He said He came to find what had been lost."

"I'm condemned… possessed by unclean spirits!"

"He is the Door to redemption."

"? …"

"Let's go, Mistress! He will receive you!"

The night swung tiny lights in the dark firmament as a boat sailed the waters in the direction of Capernaum.

The dialogue had been brief. But a whole life permeated it…

On her way back, she was no longer the same.

A strange and powerful transformation had impressed in her new hopes and ideals never dreamed before.

She felt her old self dying while listening to Him. She felt herself alive on her way home.

The next day a stunned Magdala got the news of the conversion of the sinner. She had given away everything she owned and, with only the strictly necessary, she started a new life.

"She'll come back," mocked some.

"She was always deranged!" scoffed others.

"The city will not lose her; she'll come back to the den of pleasures!" concluded the more cynical.

A few days passed…

* * *

Magdala was a city of paradox.

Rich and dazzling, it hosted those exotic and bilious characters that swarm to all cities of luxury and pleasure in all epochs.

In Magdala resided a man of strange habits named Simon, who enjoyed hosting illustrious personages that passed through the famous metropolis. A Pharisee, he was proud and zealous of traditions and liked to show off his personal wealth.

His palace had seen respectable figures of the arts and scholars, geniuses of wars and laws, priests and itinerant wizards. The banquets in which he honored them, and thus honored himself, were talked about for days in the entire city.

Simon, like all people in Magdala, had heard of Jesus. Thrilled with the notoriety of the Galilean, he thought it a great idea to receive Him in his home, to introduce Him to his friends, to speak with Him.

Perhaps, thought Simon, he was the Awaited Liberator, as he was told by a rich merchant, and it would be wise of him to become His friend, so as to also be triumphant at the time of His triumph; if He was a true Rabbi, it would be honorable for him to receive a holy man in those days of open prophetism in Israel.

Knowing that the Master was near Magdala, he sent emissaries with the auspicious invitation.

Accepting it, on the appointed day the Rabbi and two disciples, followed by the curiosity of those who swarmed the road through which they would pass, arrived at the bedecked house, greeted by smiles of joy and thinly disguised scorn.

Once inside the house, the feast started.

Guests settled comfortably on the spread out couches, obsequious servants bringing small tables with delicacies and dry fruit started to serve.

Harps, strummed softly amid slender columns, filled the ample hall with a sad melody.

The air, however, was heavy.

Simon from time to time would gaze sideways at the Stranger, who seemed remote.

The uncomfortable silence among the guests made the festivity insipid and unpleasant.

Conversations would end in monosyllabic exchanges, without much interest.

Almost at the end of the banquet screams and voices were heard in a violent altercation. Suddenly the figure of a strange, weeping and disheveled woman burst into the room.

Strands of her unkempt hair were pasted to her large forehead covered in sweat; her bulging eyes glowing intensely; her blushing cheekbones protruding like ripe apples; and her dress, completely rumpled...

She looked around, as if searching for someone, and semi-deranged she threw herself at the feet of the Rabbi, who remained impassive in His seated position.

Everything happened so fast, Simon did not have any time to take action.

He was stupefied! Yes, he knew that woman. He had visited her house before and had taken part in some nights of orgy...

A strange sensation took hold of him in a split second.

An abundant cold sweat started to drip unpleasantly.

His honorable house had received a woman of ill-repute.

He wanted to expel her. His intent was to do it. But he was fearful.

He knew her *courage*, her audacity, since she had dared to come all the way to his house…

It was Mary!

Transformed since her encounter with the Rabbi, she felt free from the seven demoniacal spirits that made her so miserable. She was another woman, entirely renewed.

How she had suffered under their yoke!

Mortifications, nameless desperations, terrible bursts of apathy and fear under their cruel clutches!

But since, on the night she had gone to see Him, His clear eyes gazed at her, she felt free.

A new joy, which she had never experienced before, pervaded her confused and suffering spirit.

She felt hopeful, although just released from the mire.

In her mind, she could still hear His words at the unforgettable encounter: "There are fragrant and immaculately white flowers that spread their perfume over the mud that secure their roots…"

She would rebuild her life. She would fight for it!

After freeing herself from the oppression of the posse of spirits, she wanted to publicly display the unequivocal signs of her rebirth.

The banquet at the house of Simon, who she knew, was her chance.

She did not hesitate. She could be expelled or even stoned. She had nothing to fear. If necessary to pay for her guilt with blood, she was ready to wash away her shame.

Infused by such thoughts, she went resolutely, her mind feverish with hope.

And now there she was. Everybody looking at her with utter disgust.

Tears flowed from her eyes and fell on His feet, which she dried with her long hair. She broke the seal of the alabaster bottle she had brought with her and poured the oil on the feet of the Rabbi, anointing them with pious affection. The rare perfume filled the room while she continued with her generous gesture.

He did not say anything, as if He felt nothing.

The meal ended coldly. The rest of the guests made it a point to not hide their simulated embarrassment.

With clenched teeth, an irate Simon grumbled:

"This man, if he were a prophet, would certainly know who and what kind of woman is this, who is touching him: that she is a sinner."

His pure eyes gazed around serenely, and then He spoke with a calm and gentle voice:

"Simon! I have something to tell you."

"Say it, Master."

"A certain creditor had two debtors: one owed five hundred denarii, and the other fifty. And since they did not have the ability to repay him, he forgave them both. So then, which of them loves him more?"

Simon smiled for the first time. He was astute, skillful in business. Urged into a direct conversation, he happily replied:

"I suppose that it is he to whom he forgave the most."

"You have judged correctly."

The Rabbi turned His gaze towards the suffering woman and further asked Simon:

"Do you see this woman? I entered into your house. You gave me no water for my feet. But she has washed my feet with tears, and has wiped them with her hair. You gave no kiss to me. But she, from the time that she entered, has not ceased to kiss my feet. You did not anoint my head with oil. But she has anointed my feet with ointment. Because of this, I tell you: many sins are forgiven her, because she has loved much. But he who is forgiven less, loves less."

Simon was stunned. He did not understand those clear words, maybe because of the impact of the chaotic emotions erupting in his tormented and pusillanimous spirit.

His eyes inordinately wide opened, he looked at the Rabbi.

The Master stood up and offering his hands to the woman, He said gently:

"Your sins are forgiven ... Go in peace!"

Exuding joy, she leapt to her feet and laughing out loud, left as fast as she had come in.

Afterwards, she disappeared from Magdala.

Every afternoon, however, amid the crowds, helping sick children, offering her sight to the blind and her hands to the disabled, repentant and anxious for her own complete renewal, she followed Jesus from city to city, wherever He went...

A few days ago, she had joyously entered Jerusalem with the rest of the Galileans.

But there was such sorrow in Him as he rode the donkey into the city that she became sad as well.

* * *

She continued to recall the last events in her distressed mind.

The betrayal of Judas, His imprisonment, the arbitrary judgment, the climbing towards the Place of the Skull...

She would have given her life to lessen His sufferings.

When, along with the other women who followed Him she saw Him fall, she had run to support Him.

He, stoic and sublime as always, spoke to them through bruised and wounded lips:

"Daughters of Jerusalem, do not weep over me. Instead, weep over yourselves and over your children. For behold, the days will arrive in which they will say, 'Blessed are the barren, and the wombs that have not borne, and the breasts that have not nursed.' Then they will begin to say to the mountains, 'Fall over us,' and to the hills, 'Cover us.' For if they do these things with green wood, what will be done with the dry?"

Mocking laughter roared through the crowd...

And finally the dolorous hour of the Cross.

Amid His Mother's tears, He had conveyed the legacy of universal fraternity, entrusting her to John and John to her.

He, however, was left on the wood of infamy.

Next to His Mother, looking at Him in His last moments, extremely debilitated as His life withered away, she feared she would lose her mind. But that's when she noticed that the cross, the traditional symbol for punishment, after Him had turned into an eloquent route to sublimation: a bridge towards Immortality.

As His head slumped down, she wished to once more embrace His feet and kiss them gently, but was unable to move...

* * *

She opened her swollen eyes, sore from weeping at these memories.

"Be strong, my child!" The Blessed Mother tenderly said to her. "Our sorrows are with Him now."

"I saw Him, Mother!" She stammered.

"I believe you, my daughter. I do believe. I know that my Son lives!"

* * *

The days now went by filled with longing and remembrance. She returned with her companions to the simple and gentle Galilee, to the restless waters of the sea He had loved so much.

The terrible words her inconsiderate companion had lashed against her continued to mentally hound her.

In Galilee He reappeared and talked extensively to all of them – almost five hundred – urging them to proclaim His "sayings" and the edification of the Kingdom of light in the frontiers of the spirit.

"Go forth and teach all nations…"

"In the world, you will have difficulties …"

"Remember me, I have overcome the world…"

"Behold, I am sending you like sheep…"

All these new teachings resonated in the air…

Yesterday, the news from the travelers to Emmaus, today the outstanding fishing … Absent, He had never been so close, filling the hearts with His unmistakable presence.

It was the ministry that had just begun for them…

Forty days after the terrible events, He appeared to His Mother and the Eleven, who were all in Jerusalem, and led them to Bethany. They followed Him eager and joyously as in the bygone days…

The journey, however, was not the same as before. There was happiness among them, but also fear. The joy of the reunion and the fear of the weakness they had displayed.

Arriving at the summit of the mountain, with the resplendent city at their feet, they asked:

"Lord, is this the time when you will restore the kingdom of Israel?"

The Master looked at them with the same sorrow of the past. His friends still did not understand what His Kingdom was, a kingdom with neither geographical dimensions nor politics, a kingdom extended beyond the galaxies of the firmament...

He replied with a tone of supreme comprehension:

"It is not yours to know the times or the moments, which the Father has set by his own authority."

And to the collective wordless question, he responded:

"But you shall receive the power of the Holy Spirit, passing over you, and you shall be witnesses for me in Jerusalem, and in all Judea and Samaria, and even to the ends of the earth."

All eyes were fixed on Him, and only then did they perceive that He was slowly ascending, His hands stretched towards them in a gesture of caress, His garments luminous, until He disappeared into the heights...

After tyrannical struggles with herself, she experienced loneliness and abandonment after all the others went on to preaching and living the Message.

Alone with herself, wandering the long shores that reminded her of Him, she met lepers who came from afar to seek help from His hands. But since they were late, she embraced them as brothers and sisters and went with them to the valley of the unclean, singing songs of joy...

* * *

Transformed and renewed from the moment she had encountered Him, she died at the gates of the city of Ephesus, ascending to Life in the arms of Jesus. Mary of Magdala, the woman whose experience and complete love for the Master are living lessons that have crossed the centuries...

CHAPTER 18

GO AND CONQUER THE WORLD

A deep longing lingered in the air.[61]

Everything in Galilee evoked memories: the scenery of the immense, generous, fish-abundant chanting sea that He had loved so much; the riverside towns adorned in green hedges with bountiful orchards; the uplands crowned with wheat, which had inspired His unmistakable parables!... Everything there, in the bucolic region of the simple souls of the people, bore the seal of His gentleness. Even the serene mountains worn down by the winds, the Sun and the rains seemed to remember Him! The Jordan River, the cantilena of its murmuring waters carrying salt to the Dead Sea, likewise evoked Him! Every corner in that beloved Galilee of simple loves and passionate people, of fervent faith and hearts of children, kept the living marks of His trajectory. He had walked its roads, He had framed its scenery with the most touching expressions of affection.

---

[61] Acts 1-2. – Spirit Auth.

Canaan had seen the amazing phenomenon of the transformation of water into wine; Magdala, the former place of the tormented woman He had freed, had sheltered Him more than once; Naim had been the site of the recovery of the child, apparently dead; Capernaum, Tiberias, Nazareth, the little towns of Samaria, all of them carried memories of Him, impregnated with His presence.

In Judea, with rare exceptions, the evocative scenes of the betrayal, the Passion, solitude, imprisonment, torture, death... and resurrection!

However, it was in captivating, endearing and unassuming Galilee that He had chosen to ascend, next to that unforgettable sea, at sunset... His disciples were all Galileans but one, Judas, born in Kerioth in Judea...

Jerusalem now seemed more cruel, its air more difficult to breathe.

Designated to that location, they remained in the city, almost one hundred and twenty out of the "five hundred brethren," the living witnesses of His ascension...

Those closest to Him frequently gathered in the Cenacle, where a few lived, waiting for answers to ease their concerns.

Despite their communion with the Rabbi, fully aware of their insecurities, they did not feel prepared for the ministry.

Until recently they had been encouraged by the unexpected encounters with Him, the continued news, the visions, the incomparable dialogues...

Plunged into irrepressible longing, they felt disheartened, not knowing how or where to start.

They recognized their inexperience and limitations.

They did not even attempt to reorganize the group, now short of one since the desertion of Judas, their mislead brother...

Jerusalem was a polyglot city.

They had difficulty being understood or understanding others, even their compatriots.

The Hebrew language was "sacred" because the Books were written in Hebrew – inheritor of all traditions of the people, the language consecrated to the issues of the Lord. For them, however, simple and unlearned men, the dialect of their region was easier and more pleasing. How could they address such an enormous barrier?

They gathered to evoke Him, to discuss His deeds, to enrich themselves with pious emotion and to weep with longing, jubilant for knowing that they were chosen, but still...

* * *

The Pentecost[62] had a very special significance for the people, for the whole Israel.

They gathered on *that day* consecrated to the Fiftieth with a festive spirit.

Through superior inspiration, Matthias had joined the Apostolic College after the "casting of lots," his selection approved unanimously.

On that particular day they missed the Master more than on any previous days. They shared a feeling that *something* was about to happen.

---

[62] For the Jews, the Pentecost celebrates the day Moses received the *Tables of the Law* on Mt. Sinai. Initially it was consecrated to translate gratitude to the Lord for the blessings to the people. Among the Christians, it recalls the coming down of the "Voices from Heaven" in the Cenacle fifty days after Easter. Easter, on its turn, reminds the Jews of the exodus from Egypt and is celebrated on the fourteenth day of the first moon of their religious year. Among the Christians, it evokes the Resurrection of Jesus. – Spirit Auth.

The city was swarming with pilgrims.

The street bustle reached the enclosed cenacle where they had gathered.

Their hearts were beating with indefinable emotions.

Suddenly "there came a sound from heaven, like that of a wind approaching violently, and it filled the entire house where they were sitting. And there appeared to them separate tongues, as if of fire, which settled upon each one of them. And they were all filled with the Holy Spirit. And they began to speak in various languages…"

It seemed like scales had fallen from their eyes, the mental gloom had been lifted. A vigorous discernment permeated them all, lucidity and confidence bursting forth in words initially hesitant, but soon flowing from their lips as if they were experiencing a singular ecstasy.

Guided by an incontrollable impulse they opened the windows, rushed out the door, speaking but not knowing about what or the reason for the words and expressions that were strange to them.

Mentally they had the impression of sailing softly beyond inscrutable rivers they had never glided over before.

Soft breezes ran through, hearts beat faster, overtaken by indescribable bliss. Bulging veins on temples could barely contain blood circulation. Eyes bright and glassy, a mortal paleness, abundant sweating, and words pouring out in cascades under a strange and vigorous command.

Drawn by the unusual event, passersby approached; their curiosity aroused, they started to inquire about it.

Onlookers were visitors from the provinces and from faraway lands: "Parthians and Medes and Elamites, and those who inhabit Mesopotamia, Judea and Cappadocia, Pontus and Asia, Phrygia and Pamphylia, Egypt and the parts of Libya which are around Cyrene, and new arrivals of the Romans, likewise Jews and new converts, Cretans and Arabs"... and all heard them announcing in their "own languages the mighty deeds of God. And they were all astonished, and they wondered, saying to one another: But what does this mean?"

"Behold, are not all of these who are speaking Galileans? And how is it that we have each heard them in our own language, into which we were born?"

Scorn and commotion ensues, and after the first few moments someone mocks: "These men are full of new wine!"

Laughter and taunting from the rowdier threatened further:

"Let's put an end to all this chatter."

The disciples, however, in trance, under the direct influence of Superior Spirits, the Ambassadors of Jesus, continued to preach, transfigured, thus initiating the New Era of the Immortal Spirit already launched by the Resurrected Rabbi.

The "Voices from Heaven" had descended and mediumship had enabled the perfect communion with Immortality. The "Church Triumphant" raising in the hearts the "Church Militant." The Consoler emerging as a prelude of the distant future where one day it would bring back to the world and its disturbed humankind the message of life, the true rebirth of the pure, prophetic, and regenerating Christianity.[63]

Xenoglossy,[64] bursting forth from the followers of the Crucified Master, astonished the listeners.

---

[63] With Allan Kardec, the Consoler was able to structure the guidelines that now, in Spiritism, reproduce the untarnished message of the Gospel and its lofty principles. – Spirit Auth.

[64] Xenoglossy: polyglot mediumship. Glossolalia: speaking in an unknown language. – Spirit Auth.

The disciples continued to speak in tongues, immune to the jeering, when Simon, visibly in trance, his face irradiating a soft light, stepped forward and spoke eloquently to the crowd.

He did not resemble the former man of the sea.

He was no longer the fisherman of silvery waters, skillfully handling his old fishing nets. His words, his heart were now a sublime fishing net and vessel in the sea of hope. His was a new type of fishing: that of human beings for the Kingdom of God.

* * *

Standing tall, confident, with a steady voice he said:

"Men of Judea, and all those who are staying in Jerusalem ..."

The fervent words resonated with strength and beauty.

Mentally he saw himself back at Mount Tabor, recalling the transfiguration of the Master. The unforgettable scene penetrated his mind with incoercible celerity. His eyes teared up at the psychic vision of the Master, accompanied by Moses and Elijah, in resplendent garments...

Warm tears rolled down the face furrowed by so many struggles.

With unmistakable eloquence, he continued:

"Let this be known to you, for these men are not inebriated, as you suppose, for it is the third hour[65] of the day. But this is what was spoken of by the prophet Joel:"

---

[65] Between 8 am to 9 am. – Tr.

"And this shall be: in the last days, says the Lord,
I will pour out, from my Spirit, upon all flesh;
and your sons and your daughters shall prophesy.
And your youths shall see visions,
and your elders shall dream dreams...
And certainly, upon my men and women servants in those days,
I will pour out from my Spirit,
and they shall prophesy'..."

He paused. There was complete silence. A natural respect had set in and the transparent air left the bright blue of the skies exposed.

The Galileans remembered the places where Jesus had preached, the red anemones tinting the dark-green fields...

"'And I will bestow wonders in heaven above,
and signs on earth below...
The sun shall be turned into darkness
and the moon into blood
before the great and manifest day of the Lord arrives!
And this shall be: whoever shall invoke the name of the
Lord will be saved.'"

"'Men of Israel, hear these words: Jesus of Nazareth is a man confirmed by God among you'... We all saw the *prodigies* in the sowing of the Truth by this Ambassador and Excellent Son of God. After the contemptible crucifixion imposed by our folly, He resuscitated from the dead and appeared to us, choosing us to keep alive and clear the sun of His love in the journey of spirits. 'Therefore let all the house of Israel know beyond a doubt that God has made this Jesus whom you crucified both Lord and Christ.' Reflect and repent, freeing yourselves from the hyenas of greed, anger and all the passions that follow you famished and pitilessly…"

The words rose, lofty and unparalleled, its modulation infusing spirits and hearts.

Those who listened, enraptured, were touched, as if transformed into living harps played by invisible hands of uncommon skill.

Moved, many gathered around him, anxious and thirsty for peace, letting themselves be led by the imponderable vibrations as the cadence of words ended in a touching peroration.

The impressive breath of peace lingered in the immediate surroundings.

The joys of that moment resonated deeply inside everyone.

* * *

Henceforth, the Spirits of Light would lead them through the paths of this world, raising the fallen, consoling the afflicted, freeing the possessed, preaching and spreading the light, all of them, in truth like the Master Himself had done.

From there they would go, as they did, all over the earth, singing and living the lofty song of the Good Tidings, which now are vibrating once more in all the corners of the world, redirecting humanity, through Jesus, the Unconquered King, back to the bosom of the Almighty.

CHAPTER 19

SIMON PETER: ROCK AND SHEPHERD

The resplendent morning seemed to vibrate with the same cheerful joy felt by them.[66]

It was their beloved Galilee.

The friendly sea, old companion of deep ponderings and long toils, rose in undulations of white foam breaking down on the pebbles of the amenable beach.

Everything sang a song of joy: the light air of dawn, the whispering breeze in the trees, the singing of the birds, the orchestration of nature… and the fervent hearts.

That was the third encounter with the Master since the tragic events in Jerusalem.

It had happened so quickly!

Anxious to regain his former agility after what had happened, he had been casting his net since night time, his mind filled with remembrances. Suddenly, he heard the unforgettable voice of the Rabbi saying: "Cast the net to the right side of the ship, and you will find some."

He did it mechanically, as in days past.

---

[66] Jn. 21:1-25. – Spirit Auth.

Pulling in the net, he became ecstatic: the abundance of fish was astounding.

Only then did he realize he was naked.

He hid from view in the rugged boat, wrapping his tunic around himself.

He then extended his gaze towards the beach and there He was: the Master Himself.

His heart beating in disarray made him dizzy, his whole being filling with an indescribable joy.

He did not wait for the boat to reach the shore. He threw himself into the waters.

When the other disciples arrived with the fish in the boat, He took one, grilled it on the embers of an improvised fire and ate with them.

"Approach and dine!" He said naturally.

The scenes of bygone days were once again repeated. The distance in time had shrunk and everything resumed as if nothing had happened.

His eyes shone even brighter, and that face, tinged in the past with melancholy, was now emanating indescribable love.

"Simon, son of Jonah, do you love me more than these?"

Yes, he loved Him! He had given himself totally to the Good Tidings since His voice called him to fish for souls in the sea of humanity. What could he, Peter, say in that moment of such lofty union?

"Yes, Lord, you know that I love You."

"Feed my lambs."

He felt weak, he knew he was weak.

To follow Him, and only for that reason, he had abandoned these shores. He had been born there, he had lived there, his whole world was located inside those narrow borders, which could be covered in one glance.

How could he tend to lambs?

"Simon, son of Jonah, do you love me?"

The question had a tinge of sorrow.

Peter looked at Him anxiously. Would it be necessary to repeat it?

"Yes, Lord, you know that I love You."

"Feed my lambs."

Immense are the pathways treaded by humankind and distant the lands they inhabit. He felt alone, weak and sad. Was the Rabbi doubting his dedication?

"Simon!"

The words seemed like the music of crystals shattering against the rocks.

"… son of Jonah, do you love me?"

"Lord, you know all things," Peter could not contain his spontaneous tears. "You know that I love You, that I gave my Life to You."

"Feed my sheep."

"I say to you, when you were younger, you girded yourself and walked wherever you wanted. But when you are older, you will extend your hands, and another shall gird you and lead you where you do not want to go." That cruel night came back to his mind, that night of insanity.

Three times the Master had asked him, and three times they had pointed at him…

"Are you not also among the disciples of this man?" asked him the girl servant at the door of the house of the High Priest.

"I am not!" he yelled back almost unconsciously.

A terrible weight came over his reddened temples. He wanted to run and scream: I not only know Him, but I also love Him. But he could not do it.

He had mingled with the crowd, his mind clouded, when the flames of the fire lighted his face and they identified him:

"Are you not also among the disciples of this man?"

A silent ire exploded in the depths of his restless spirit and he replied with resentment, unable to contain himself:

"I am not, I have never seen Him…"

Oh Heavens! He was deranged. How could he deny the Rabbi? What power commanded his weakness?

He left distressed, without the courage to overcome so much imbalance when another servant of the High Priest inquired of him:

"Did I not see you in the garden with him? Are you not His friend?"

"No," he replied with deep sorrow, "I have never seen Him!"

His pain was unbearable, now that the rooster crowed, with sadness, timing his perfidy.

He seemed to see those eyes gazing at him with sadness.

He, Peter, had said some time before: "I will give my life to You."

"The rooster will not crow this day, until you have three times denied that you know me."

The modulation of His voice had been unforgettable.

He had found that impossible. How could the Master predict such a harsh and reprehensible demise of his faithfulness?

But he had indeed denied Him three times, although he loved Him.

He knew he was weak, but he never thought to be weak to the point of betraying, fleeing, and denying!

He did not ignore the interference of the *"powers of evil."* The Master had referred to them many times, urging prayer and vigilance.

He knew they would be the target a thousand times of such attacks. However, it had been he, Peter, who had succumbed, briefly taken over by them, as an example of incomparable warning for all times.

Earlier, he had fallen asleep in the Garden, succumbing to a strange exhaustion...

... And could it be by any chance that these three questions posed by Him were meant to strengthen the ties to his duties in his mind?

The Rabbi stood up and began to instruct him as to the dedication necessary towards the sheep lost in the challenging pathways of the earth.

It meant detaching himself from all other passions and to *die* to all types of expectations, keeping one passion only: to sacrifice himself for the happiness of everybody else.

John certainly would be spared. He would be left to sing the Message with the melodious vibration of his beautiful example, as a divine harp played by a vigorous unknown hand.

He, however, would be slated to shed bitter tears and retrace the pathways, until other hands would seize his hands and tie them with ropes...

He exulted inwardly.

A powerful, strange power emanating from the Benefactor infused him.

Suddenly he understood everything he had not grasped before.

Sweetness and gentleness penetrated him. Of an austere moral temperament, he felt emphatic and tender at that very moment and would do everything to stay that way...

His mind rejoicing, he recalled the last almost three years of familiarity. They felt like a course the Master had come to teach them, all simple and ignorant disciples. And the last days, where He seemed Absent but they felt Him powerfully Present, denoted the intensive training for the work of communion with humanity.

"Who do they say is the Son of Man?" He recalled the eloquent question with which He had honored them some months ago.

"Some say John the Baptist" they answered with certainty, "others say Elijah; and still others, Jeremiah or one of the prophets reincarnated…"

"But you, who do you say I am?"

The colorful day, golden with sun, was a canvass of incomparable beauty, a musical sheet waiting for the notes of an unmistakable melody.

"I say that 'You are the Christ, the living Son of God', the One we are all waiting for…"

It was as if a strange voice had spoken with his voice, through his mouth…

"Blessed are you, Simon son of Jonah. For flesh and blood has not revealed this to you."

"I also say to you, Peter, that upon this rock, upon this truth that you just proclaimed I will build My Church, the Church of truth and revelation of the Invisible World, because it was not you that spoke but the Father who is in Heaven… And the forces of evil will not prevail against it, because it is the Church of the Revelation of the Truth."

He had spoken with the breath of the Father, had become a messenger of the On High.

The disciples looked at him very moved, and even the humble wild flowers of the fields released their fragrance, scenting the air.

Soon after, however, assailed by a sudden fear of the torture the Master would suffer, he started to reprimand Him for saying such things, to the point of the Master having to admonish him:

"Get behind me, Satan; you are an obstacle to me. For you are not behaving according to what is of God, but according to what is of men."

Without understanding, he had asked Him what happened, to which He explained:

"It is necessary to be watchful. When you spoke about me you were a messenger of the Unfading Light, but then you let yourself be an agent of the Darkness."

At that moment he understood the duality between good and evil, the unceasing struggle that so much concerned the Master.

Death, not extinguishing life, is a vehicle that takes those that it harvests as they are, with what they have acquired, remaining as they were, in the way they preferred while in the physical world...[67]

He had gotten to know the Rabbi when life disenchantments were first starting to gray his hair.

Accustomed to the toils of the sea, he had learned to respect the Law and the Prophets. However, he understood very little the subtleties and discussions that filled the entire time at the Synagogue, the arguments utilized to persecute and censure those who were already afflicted and tormented.

He knew well the priests and the Levites. Their garments were white, but their hearts and spirits were dark and filthy.

He followed the cold duties of religious worship as a habit, devoid of any emotion; but he loved the suffering people of the riverside villages and squares, the beaches and the roads, people like him, also suffering and without any hope.

---

[67] Read more in "The return from the corporeal to the spirit life" (*The Spirits' Book*, Allan Kardec, published by the International Spiritist Council). – Tr.

When the Rabbi glanced His eyes over the pain of the multitudes, and His voice beckoned hope on the beautiful beach calling out for him, he had stood up to follow Him, forgetting everything else.

He only went back to fishing during the intervals of the ministry or to help his companions with the needs of the group.

All those nights had been filled with hope, and all the days marked with light.

All the small misunderstandings among the group, the Rabbi knew how to settle them.

"What were you discussing on your way here?" He continued to remember His words. Those were already His last days.

"Were you discussing," asked the Master with sorrow as He waited for them, "were you discussing who among you is the greatest before me? But I tell you that the greatest shall be the servant of all others…"

What a strange and profound lesson! What perceptiveness from the Rabbi!

He recalled the vision of the lake and his fear, the pacified storm, the payment of the tribute … all evocations miraculously fresh in his overexcited mind.

How difficult it had been up to now to understand the subtleties of His message.

He was indeed *Cephas*, *Petra*, pebble or rock, surely a thick head. He had not possessed the sensitivities for the things of the spirit.

Pebble or rock, as the Master nicknamed him, would that mean that his faith and self-denial would be comparable to the strength and solidity of the rock? He could not tell.

Since the Resurrection, however, his thoughts became clearer and his remembrances gave him greater lucidity.

"We left everything to follow You. What will we profit from it?" That was the coarse man.

"Explain to us this parable." That was the sign of ignorance being lifted.

"Teach us how to pray." That was the rock starting to receive the light.

On the Tabor, he selfishly suggested that tents be erected for them...

"Yes, Lord, you know how much I love You," expressed the desire to remain faithful to Him and to follow Him...

Now he felt His wisdom illuminating his love, differentiating the trivial from the sublime, the deeply-felt from the superficial.

"I will follow You..."

"Simon, son of Jonah, do you love me?" The question finally resonated within him:

"Yes, you know that I love You!"

From now on he was inescapably bounded to the Rabbi, delivered to His sheep.

Some days later he saw His ascension amid tears of longing and profound gratitude.

From Bethany he went to Jerusalem to tend to the sheep of His flock...

* * *

In the "Mansion of the Way,"[68] or on the road to Joppa, or in Antioch, in the "Mediterranean world," or in Rome, the

---

[68] "Simon had been at the center of a great humanitarian movement. ... It was for this reason that Peter's residence, donated by a group of friends of the Way, was overflowing with the sick and the hopeless forsaken." (*Paul and Stephen*, by Spirit Author Emmanuel, International Spiritist Council, 2008). – Tr.

venerable figure of Simon Peter was the corner stone of the Church of Jesus for Humankind. He was the emeritus herald of the endeavors of faith and hope until the moment when, in "Babylon," with Paul, while increasing and upholding the horizons of the living faith, "other hands tied his hands"... and led him towards his ultimate testimony. He was the disciple par excellence – Simon Peter: rock and shepherd – who lifted himself from his illusions and errors to live Jesus until the last moment, tending to the sheep of His flock of love...

CHAPTER 20

JESUS

"And when I have been lifted up from the earth, I will draw all things to myself."

Jn. 12:32.

As the rays of the Sun streamed their golden hue, bathing Nature in an incomparable feast of light, the last words were said, the final and meaningful instructions were given, and the course of the tasks for the future delineated. Haloed in indefinable light, He slowly ascended amid the explosion of tears of his disciples and the hopes of redemption by means of their work thereafter.

The mountain in Bethany grew smaller, the horizons of the world grew bigger, His eyes tenderly gazing over the fertile field of work where, under His inspiration, the flowers of love should blossom throughout the times.

He had lived with these simple folk, establishing the basis for the fraternal edification for the spirits.

He had made Himself smaller to minister humility, and had descended to earth to better serve.

He had dispensed with any intermediaries to realize His plans and He Himself had come to participate in all preparatory details – each and every day and every moment with the utmost dedication, so as to infuse through example the firm lessons of duty and abnegation.

Anticipating the political, social, and spiritual consequences of His message in the History of all times, He was able to foresee the legions of those who would accept sacrifice and torture, remaining faithful to the postulates of the Truth all the way to an opprobrious death ...

The thought of their faithfulness brought the Rabbi unusual elation.

The conquistadors prepared soldiers and mercenaries, instilling terror, utilizing war strategies supported by impiety, espionage, and betrayal. They combated physical bodies, pillaging cities, smothering the aspirations of weakened peoples...

He had arrived anonymously and departed trampled underfoot. But He had legated to those who remained confident the armor of patience, the weapons of love, the strategy of the incessant and indefatigable good.

The field, perhaps often, would be littered with corpses... the corpses of his legionaries, giving themselves in sacrifice but without ever sacrificing others.

He had offered them the tools, unknown until then, of conciliation and gentleness, and had launched a strange and peculiar revolutionary mode: the non-violent combat.

For this reason, apparently there had been no place for Him on the earth ... Nonetheless, blessings sprouted from the living and incorruptible lessons of His love, and the handful of Spirits who stayed behind in their physical bodies gradually would attain the unmovable high objectives to be achieved afterwards.

They were only a humble pollen, but one which would fertilize the whole earth, surpassing distances and time.

In the infinite of the hours, the moment would arrive for the final communion with these beloved souls and the complete triumph over the miseries that agitated minds and hearts.

He thought about the men and women pulled from their daily chores for the incomparable journey of fraternal assistance. They had not fully perceived the profound meaning of "leaving everything behind to follow Him." For months they nurtured strange and naïve hopes, quarreling amongst themselves for precedence, dreaming about imaginary triumphs, aspiring to trivial honors… Now, slowly, after the questions that perturbed their ability to reason and clouded their hesitant sentiments had finally been clarified, they were able to sense the lofty responsibility they were ultimately invested with.

They would depart into the world like a discreet fragrance of potent penetration, and wherever they passed, without noticing it they would leave indelible marks.

To a woman used to silk cushions and seduction He had offered valor and strength, so that, renewed, she would become a living example of the victory of the spirit over putrescible flesh.

He had touched a "doctor of the Law," enabling his deeper understanding of the complex mechanism of purifying rebirths.

He had made known to a faithful administrator the hopes of the Kingdom, giving him back his sick daughter, in an eloquent acknowledgment of the value of spiritual health…

With His simple words and unassuming attitudes, He had confounded the hypocrites and liars, the deceivers and those who delighted in the misuse of things of all nature.

His friends, His inner circle of all hours, He had chosen them among the modest occupations of the people, nurturing them in a regime of austere discipline and incessant affection for the interminable struggles of a dedication without limits…

He knew that, sweaty and stumbling, but resolute and consciously, they would carry His voice to all spirits, alleviating the terrible wounds that raged in humanity's organism.

The hands of greed and criminality would rise, all types of turpitude would be enlisted, the most villainous weapons would be utilized, but they would stay faithful to Him while crossing the earth.

He could see the flames and the crosses, the beasts and the swords, the unusual cruelties and the implacable persecutions coming their way without breaking their spirits or diminishing their courage. Their sustenance was the Church of Revelation built upon the rock of Truth, with the mortar of His blood and the seal of His resurrection, leaving to the future the results of His journey for love…

The lamb would mingle with the *wolf* and chaff would give way to wheat, humankind blossoming under the blessings of complete peace.

"Glory to God in the highest, peace on earth, good will toward men," angelic voices sang, greeting the Supreme King arriving at the throne of the On High.

The Divine Friend – well beyond the sphere of darkness where human beings were left wrapped in their passions and anxieties, their spirits lacking confidence – opened his arms and in complete harmony, thinking on those who would follow Him throughout the times, whispered:

"Father, Thou art in Heaven"… as He returned to the bosom of the One who had sent Him, without forsaking, however, the workers on the terrestrial arena "until the end of time."

* * *

Since then pain and suffering have found relief through hands that were weak but have become strong in contact with Christian work.

Wherever the hydra of war passes through, sowing corpses and destruction, selfless hearts will follow, tending to widows, orphans, abandonment, and misery.

Impiety no longer took primacy on the earth, nor did persecution achieve its purpose.

He has been present everywhere, the simple mention of His name a vigorous stimulus for liberty and peace of spirit.

Not triumphant in the world, Jesus defeated all vicissitudes and established the principles for the New World of the Happy Humanity, in whose construction we are all united together, the incarnate and the discarnate, in the practice of evangelical learning and living.

AFTERWORD

The Gospel – the tidings or the good tidings – is the most expressive story of a life, through other lives, illuminating the lives of all humankind. It is the story of a Man who rises in History and becomes larger than History, dividing it with His birth, becoming the resplendent framework of the respository of universal thought.

This – the most remarkable story ever told – is condensed in the "New Testament," a modest Work of a little more than three hundred and fifty pages. Written by two personal witnesses of all events, Matthew and John; confirmed by the testimony of others who lived with Him, namely Peter – who asks Mark to write it down for the recently converted Romans; compiled for the great masses of converted gentiles by Luke, the Evangelist, who received his information from Paul – the one called on the road to Damascus – and also from Mary, the Mother of Jesus, Joanna of Chuza and Mary Magdalene, among others. Further testimonies of those familiar with the events and direct participants reappear in the Letters and culminate in the visions of the Apocalypse.

In all, twenty-seven little books, comprised of two hundred chapters and seven thousand nine hundred and fifty-seven verses, in a simple narrative: four evangelical accounts, one Acts of the Apostles (attributed to Luke), fourteen Epistles by Paul,[69] one by James the Less, two by Peter, three by John, one by Judas (Thaddeus), and John's Apocalypse.

Discussed and examined for centuries, they were settled at the Council of Trent (1545-1553). It recognized their authenticity after verification of the historical documents, comprised of fragments of the first copies utilized by the resolute Christians that followed the disciples who had founded the now flourishing churches...

Despite small differences between the four evangelists' narratives – the uncontested proof of the writers' personal opinions – the story of the *Son of Man* is one and the same.

Matthew (Levi) wrote for the Israelites who became Christians, comparing the Good Tidings with the Ancient Texts, making use of images common to Hebrew thought.[70]

Mark (also called John) was the son of Mary from Jerusalem, in whose house the early Christians would gather and where the Apostle Peter, freed from prison, sought shelter. Mark had accompanied Paul and Barnabas in their apostolic work, but departed their company in Perga, Pamphylia, returning to Jerusalem. Later on, Mark was convened by Peter himself for the Christian work in Rome, at which time he wrote his gospel.[71]

Luke, newly converted by Paul, lived in Caesarea, in the home of Deacon Philip. From Philip he heard, movingly, the oral narrative of the events. In Jerusalem, the same facts were confirmed to him by James the Less. Erudite, born in

---

[69] The Epistle to the Hebrews was attributed to Paul at the Council of Trent, while the Council of Carthage considered it to be from an unknown author. We prefer the former conclusion. – Spirit Auth.

[70] Papias (75-150 AD) [bishop of Hieropolis, in Phrygia] stated that Matthew presents in his Gospel "the sayings of the Lord." – Spirit Auth.

[71] Mark, who served as an interpreter for Peter, registered with accuracy – albeit not in sequence – the words and deeds of Jesus. – Spirit Auth.

Antioch, from a Hellenic culture, Luke is the enthralled and moved narrator of the deeds and words of Jesus. It is the most beautiful of the four Gospels, infused with the gentleness of the Lamb of God. Writing to the "most excellent Theophilus," it is dedicated to the large flock of the gentiles, captivated by the fervent oratory of Paul, his master.[72] He would later write the Acts of the Apostles in his unmistakable style.

John, the beloved disciple, mystic par excellence, wrote for the Christians who already knew the Message profoundly. He went even further with his revelations to include the dialogue, in which he possibly participated as a listener, of the Master with Nicodemus and the *new rebirth*. He starts his account with the transcendental question of the Verb, and ends it with the Apocalypse and the effulgent vision of a freed *New Jerusalem*. His is the spiritual gospel.

Initially written in the language spoken by Jesus, the *Aramaic* – with the likely exception of Luke – the Gospels were soon translated into Greek, embodying the thought of the Master that would be spread over the entire world...

The most moving story ever written.
The greatest love the world has ever known.
The highest example that ever existed.
The life of Jesus is the enduring appeal towards meekness, dignity, love, and truth.
To love Him is to start to live Him.
To know Him is to inscribe Him in mind and heart.
The life that holds the story of our life – the Life of Jesus!
The perennial joy, the exceptional message of elation – the Gospel!

---

[72] Dante affirmed that Luke was "the scribe of the gentleness of Jesus." – Spirit Auth.

Made in the USA
Columbia, SC
29 January 2019